If You Could Be My Friend

If You Could Be My Friend

Letters of
Mervet Akram Sha'ban and Galit Fink

PRESENTED BY LITSA BOUDALIKA

History and Glossary by Ariel Cohen

Orchard Books • New York

Thanks to the parents of Galit and Mervet,
to Maguy Kraentzel, Shlomo Elbaz, Jawdat Manaa, Norma Marcos,
Marie-Pascale Lescot, Elisabeth Lambert, Martine Archambault

Copyright © 1992 by Gallimard Publications
Translation copyright © 1998 by Orchard Books
Translated from the French by Alison Landes
First American edition 1998 published by Orchard Books
First published in France in 1992 by Gallimard Publications
under the title *Si Tu Veux Être Mon Amie*, with translation by Ariane Elbaz and
Beatrice Khadige

Orchard Books, 95 Madison Avenue, New York, NY 10016

Manufactured in the United States of America
Book design by Mina Greenstein
The text of this book is set in 11.5 point New Baskerville.
1   3   5   7   9   10   8   6   4   2

Library of Congress Cataloging-in-Publication Data
Sha'ban, Mervet Akram.
[Si tu veux être mon amie. English]
If you could be my friend : letters of Mervet Akram Sha'ban and Galit Fink /
presented by Litsa Boudalika ; translated by Ariane Elbaz and Beatrice
Khadige ; historical overview and glossary by Ariel Cohen.   p.   cm.
Summary: Contains the correspondence between two girls, one an Israeli and
the other a Palestinian, from August 1988 until their meeting in April 1991.
Includes a brief history of their two peoples, bibliographical references,
and an index.
ISBN 0-531-30113-3 (alk. paper).—ISBN 0-531-33113-X (lib. bdg. : alk. paper)
1. Intifada, 1987- —Personal narratives, Palestinian—Juvenile literature.
2. Sha'ban, Mervet Akram—Correspondence—Juvenile literature. 3. Intifada,
1987- —Personal narratives, Israeli—Juvenile literature. 4. Fink, Galit—Correspondence—Juvenile literature. [1. Intifada, 1987- 2. Sha'ban, Mervet
Akram.   3. Fink, Galit. 4. Arab-Israeli conflict—1973–1993.]
I. Fink, Galit. II. Boudalika, Litsa. III. Title.
DS119.75.S4413   1998   956.9405'4—dc21   98-15413

To Jean Luc

We loved each other here
Different than the reality
The newspapers shrieked like the wounded.
Behind their giant headlines
We hid together.

—YEHUDA AMIHAÏ

CONTENTS

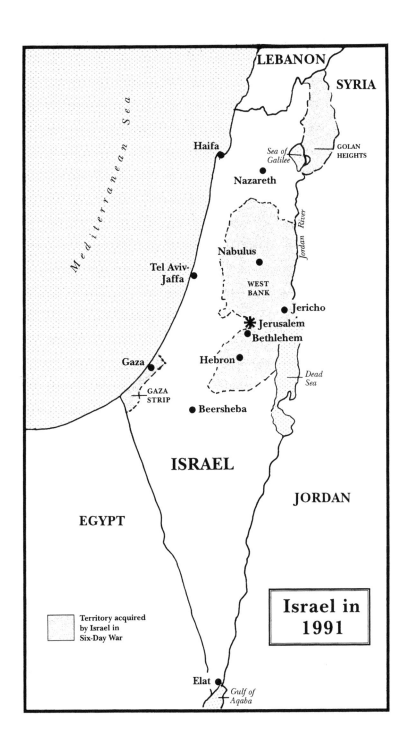

Mediterranean Sea

LEBANON

SYRIA

Haifa

Sea of
Galilee

GOLAN
HEIGHTS

Nazareth

Jordan River

Nabulus

Tel Aviv-
Jaffa

WEST
BANK

Jericho

Jerusalem
Bethlehem

Hebron

Gaza

Dead
Sea

GAZA
STRIP

Beersheba

ISRAEL

JORDAN

EGYPT

Territory acquired
by Israel in
Six-Day War

Israel in
1991

Elat

Gulf of
Aqaba

INTRODUCTION

December 24, 1987

"How long are you going away for? Is it for pleasure or for business? What is your occupation? Where did you buy this ticket? Do you have family there? What are the names of your friends in Israel? What is their address? Did you pack your own suitcase? When? Were you given any packages to bring to a parent or a friend in Israel? Do you know why we are asking you these questions?"

My interrogation by Israeli security forces lasts two and a half hours in the departure lounge of Orly Airport in Paris. The airline agents come one after the other to ask me the same questions in different order. They are obliged by security. Their suspicion irritates me. My annoyance clashes with them. The search of my bags extends to a minute examination of the contents of my toothpaste tube and my camera case. Finally, they are declared "innocent"! I am the last passenger to board the Airbus for Tel Aviv, and I complain. The security officer retorts that I am the reason the flight is late.

I have learned my first lesson for the tourist headed to Eretz Yisrael, the land of Israel. Danger haunts this country.

While the plane flies over the Alps and then the Mediterranean, I remember my grandmother's stories of pilgrimages to the Holy Land, of the mystery that the miracles she believed in evoked in me, a little girl. I realize that since that time I have kept an image of this part of the world that is religiously biblical and serene, and that clashes with the truth as it is painted on the front page of the newspapers.

Once I have disembarked in Tel Aviv and have distanced myself from Ben Gurion Airport, I finally find the mythical scenes of my imagination: a horizon of white stones strewn with bushes and stands of forests at the foot of Mount Carmel. In my mind, I re-create the journeys of the Bible, which I have read. The names on the road signs spark my dreams. On my map of Israel I measure the distances to the places I plan to visit: Saint John of Acre, Tel Aviv, Tiberias, Jerusalem, Bethlehem. . . . But the war reasserts itself when, alongside the road, I spot a rusted armored car.

"What do you expect? In this region, we are a handful of people surrounded by Arabs. Since 1948, they have started four wars against us. Luckily we've won them all. We can't trust them; all they want is to push us into the sea!" the Israeli taxi driver grumbled as he drove me to Jerusalem.

During this first visit when the War of the Stones—the Palestinian revolt against Israeli occupation—was in full swing, I realize the majority of Israelis whom I meet are overwhelmed with these concerns. The grievances are no less real on the Palestinian side: "Real Nazis, that's how they treat us. For forty years we have been less than nothing in our own land. Our children have no future. Don't you find it normal that they end up rebelling? We have nothing left to lose."

For three months I visited first Palestinians, then Israelis. They are both right and wrong at the same time. When I try to point out their prejudices or question their fears, they blame my naiveté on the fact that I am a foreigner.

In effect, I am a stranger. Neither Jewish, nor Arab, I have, nevertheless, an impression of déjà vu in the face of this conflict. In my native country, the secular hatred of the Greeks against the Turks is cultivated from the earliest age. However, for centuries, strange similarities have emerged from the culture of each of these people.

The War of the Stones, which the Palestinians have declared against the State of Israel, is called the *intifada* by both sides. Faithful to my naiveté, I continue to pick up similarities between the two cultures. I have eaten hummus, a sort of paste of mashed chickpeas, with the Israelis and with the Palestinians. The word for child has the exact same roots in both languages (in Hebrew, *yeled;* in Arabic, *walad*).

I read, I learn, I discuss. Israel-Palestine equals one land for two peoples. An equation that is accepted by a number of pacifists and intellectuals in both camps but rejected by a majority of the public and by the Israeli government[†]. Knowledge of this region's recent history opens my eyes to the complexity of the conflict that tears two peoples apart. In the meantime, I wait for examples of a dialogue between these two universes.

†At the time this was written, both Israeli and Palestinian leaders rejected the idea of a shared land. Presently, both are trying to work out a peace based on shared land.

Only poets find the strength to break the barriers and nourish their verses with forbidden love.

> *When he clasps her for the first time*
> *She cries with passion*
> *And fear of her neighbors.*

—Mahmoud Darwich

In this land cherished by so many cultures, all groups want to remain inviolate. The rare Jewish-Arab couples often live secretly or isolated from their respective families. I found one, Sarah and Fouad. They work together and have shared an attic in an Arab house in the Old City for years, although neither of their two families is aware of their secret. This is a story I would like to tell, but I hold back. For fear of shattering a fragile love, I become a partner in their secret. Nevertheless, I had a feeling that one day the history I would choose to tell would feature individuals who, like Sarah and Fouad, would be an exception to the rule of hate.

April 1988. The torrential rains that crash down on Jerusalem each winter have ceased. The intifada has been going on for more than four months. The number of victims feeds the anxiety of one side and arouses rebellion in the other. During the first days of spring I decided to visit Dheisheh, the Palestinian refugee camp that is the nearest to Jerusalem on the southern edge of Bethlehem. My friend Jawdat took me. He was born and lived in the camp for more than twenty years. He is the only one in his family who, after his marriage, succeeded in leaving Dheisheh to set up his press bureau in Bethlehem. We crossed the camp on foot, climbing a long, narrow hill, deserted because of a general strike day in the occupied territories. Not a soul. We passed stones and a burned tire. Jawdat explained to me that the day after a riot the residents avoid going out for fear of being arrested.

We found life as soon as we crossed the threshold of his house. His mother, a woman of more than seventy years, wearing a traditional hand-embroidered dress, hugged me in her arms with great warmth. I am not a stranger. Accompanied by her son, I become one of them.

"Let's have tea at my sister's. It's the house next door," Jawdat suggested. At that moment, a swarm of children ran toward us. Jawdat introduced me to each one, but I forgot their names instantly. Discreetly they questioned their uncle, *"Yehud, yehud?"* One of the few words I understand in Arabic. I was obliged to reassure them that I am not Jewish. This did not stop them from observing me. They crouched around the adults, listening to our conversation in English, which they could not understand.

At this point the first character of my story made her entrance: Mervet. She put the tea tray on the table, gave me a luminous smile, then vanished. She reappeared two hours later. "Do you like Palestine?" she asked me in broken and rudimentary English. I answered yes. She thanked me with a song. I left

Dheisheh, carrying with me the image of this twelve-year-old girl with black curls singing "The Children of Palestine."

A short time later, I met Galit, the other heroine of my story. Her family lives in a working-class neighborhood in Jerusalem. Galit is a sweet and poised Israeli girl. When she saw me for the first time, she acknowledged me with a serious expression and returned to her work in the garden.

I continued to converse with her parents in the shade of a hundred-year-old parasol pine. Her mother, Levana, works for the government and raises her five children. Galit's father explained why he had to give up his sculpture to work in a factory, and he showed me his artist's studio. From the little window, I watched Galit, who was watering the flowers and cacti in the garden. She was wearing a white T-shirt printed with seven letters. I approached her and asked her what the inscription on the back of her shirt meant. She turned around. "Ye-ru-sha-la-im," she pronounced carefully. I asked her about it. Thanks to Galit, I learned that Jerusalem in Hebrew means "City of Peace." We continued our conversation, but as soon as I brought up the Israeli-Palestinian conflict, her smile vanished.

I thought again about Mervet. Would the intifada create a hate in the children as irreversible as in the adults? In this climate of permanent war, it hurts me to see them condemned to hate each other. *Shalom,* in Hebrew, like *salaam* in Arabic, means "peace." I realize that it is precisely this desire for peace that Galit and

Mervet share, without knowing it, without knowing each other. What if they were to meet, I wonder. . . .

"So, now you'll take me to Jerusalem," suggests a thrilled Mervet.

Two days later, I discussed it with Galit, who is also impatient. "When?" she questions me, committed to going ahead. Their reactions exceeded all my hopes. Anxious to meet each other, they promptly forgot all that separates them: their cultures, their way of life, the history of their people, and the intifada.

The best way to get to know each other is, without doubt, to start corresponding. I would be the messenger for their letters. It is this correspondence, begun in 1988, that we offer to you.

LITSA BOUDALIKA

August 9, 1988
◄◯►

It has been exactly nine months since the young Palestinians who have never lived in an independent country first challenged the powerful Israeli army. A new name has been born in the blood and the fear: the intifada*. Violence seems to be the only way the Israelis and the Palestinians can communicate. The number of victims increases, especially among the Palestinians. But the young militants of the intifada, from seven to twenty-two years old, armed with stones, have decided to rip from the Israelis what the Arab countries have failed to achieve after forty years of war: the creation of a Palestinian state.

The Israeli army discovers a secret document in East Jerusalem, the Arab part of the city: it is the text of a declaration of Palestinian independence that includes, as a solution to attaining independence, the statement that all the Israelis would be pushed into the sea. The Palestine Liberation Organization (PLO) announces the creation of a government in exile. The Israeli prime minister, Yitzhak Shamir, warns the Palestinians: "If they try to achieve their goal, they will be slamming themselves into an iron fist." The tension has reached a peak.

All words followed by an asterisk (*) are defined in the glossary.

Jerusalem
9 August 1988

My name is Galit.

I am twelve years old. I am Israeli.

It is a very strange feeling to be writing to a Palestinian.

It is like a dream, a good dream.

I want to write you all kinds of things about my life. This is what I look like: I am four and a half feet tall; I have light brown hair and dark eyes. I weigh seventy-five pounds! In my house we have five children, and I am the middle one.

We live in a little Arab house in Baka, the Jerusalem neighborhood where I was born. My mother inherited the house from her grandmother when she died, because my mother took good care of her when she was old and sick.

One day I will tell you the whole story of my family. It is a very long story with parts that are too sad for a day like today.

I saw on the map that you live less than ten miles from me. Unfortunately, it is impossible for me to come and visit you there, because everyone says it is too dangerous. Write to me. I want to know who you are.

Galit

August 15, 1988

◄o►

The Islamic new year, a major religious holiday, gives way to violence. Twenty Palestinians are wounded in clashes with the Israeli military. Seven Israeli settlers, including four children, are injured by a Molotov cocktail* thrown at their car. Israeli army officials declare a strict curfew in the occupied territories*.

Dheisheh
15 August 1988

I don't know how to speak to you.

I don't know if you want to be my friend. I know very little about your life, but I feel friendly toward you.

My name is Mervet. I am intelligent, pretty, and studious. I don't hate anyone. I like people. But more than anything I want to live free in my country, like you.

Aside from my family, no one knows that I am writing you. If the girls in my class knew it, they would hate me for having a Jewish friend. But since our school is closed, they can't ask me any questions.

In our house in Dheisheh*, life is difficult because of the intifada, but I am happy in my family. I have six brothers and sisters, and I am the second oldest. My younger brothers are so wild that I had to close myself up in my parents' room to write to you. I hear them screaming from here—they are fighting! I have to go see what the problem is.

Till next time.

Mervet

August 22, 1988

—◄o►—

Following serious clashes and an increase in the violence, the Israeli government decides to deport twenty-five Palestinians. A military helicopter deposits them on the other side of the Lebanese border in the night.

Jerusalem
22 August 1988

Dear Mervet,

It was so nice of you to answer me so quickly and with a photo too! I admit I didn't imagine you looking like that at all. I thought you wore a veil over your face. I have so much to learn about your religion and customs.

It seems to me that your little brothers are devils. Believe me, though, it is better to have little brothers than a big brother who always wins every fight.

My big brother, Ayal, is fourteen. All he knows how to do is contradict me all the time. He even dared say, "Are you crazy having an Arab friend when they throw stones at our heads?" But don't worry, I don't let him push me around.

Irit and Yael are the little ones. They, at least, are angels—except when we do the shopping. I go to get them at school at four o'clock. I also baby-sit at night when my parents go out.

My older sister is called Tally. I adore her. She lends me her Walkman and her clothes when they aren't too big for me.

Unfortunately she will be leaving soon for the army*. Then I can sleep in her bed, but she won't be here to defend me against Ayal.

My mother is named Levana, which means "moon" in Hebrew. She comes from Morocco, where my grandparents lived before coming to Israel. She works in a government press office in the personnel department. Even if she comes home late from work, she finds the time to make us the best cakes in the world.

My father works at Yerolin, a clothing factory where Arabs also work. He even told me that there are workers from your camp. He gave me an idea: why don't you take the bus one morning with them? I will come and get you at Yerolin. That way I can show you Jerusalem. I promise you it is beautiful.

I only know about the refugee camps* from television. I saw that the streets were very narrow and that the residents slept on the floor. Is it really like that?

Write back,
Galit

September 12, 1988

◄O►

While the army increases arrests in the occupied territories, one voice is heard within Israel urging the country to enter into peace talks with the Palestinians.

Abie Nathan, an Israeli peace activist, goes to Tunis to talk to Yassir Arafat, the leader of the PLO. For his initiative, he risks imprisonment. Israeli law forbids all contact with representatives of terrorist organizations such as the PLO.

Dheisheh
12 September 1988

My dear Galit,

I don't want to let you down, but I don't think I can come to Jerusalem. My father would never let me go alone. The soldiers stop all the Palestinians on the road. To tell the truth, I almost never go out of Dheisheh. Before the intifada, we sometimes went to Jericho or to the beach in Gaza. The family picnicked in my grandparents' village. We grilled liver with tomatoes, onions, and peppers. We drank tea and Coke. The grown-ups sat under a tree and talked. The children sang and danced around them. That was when I loved to jump rope, and I always had one with me. Once I went with my parents all the way to the Dead Sea*. That's all I know of Israel.

Do you understand better why it is so difficult for me to come and see you? If at least my father could bring me. . . .

My father's name is Aakram. He even speaks Hebrew. He drives the ambulance for the Bethlehem hospital.

He used to be a policeman, but he resigned because he didn't like the work. When he comes home at night later than expected, we always worry a little because, these days, you never know.

I also have a big sister, who is fifteen. Her name is Majda. She is the one who helps my mother the most at home. She washes the dishes and already knows how to make bread. I take it to the ovens at the corner of our street. My other sister is named Manaal. She was born two years after me. My father says she is the most beautiful one in the family because she has big blue eyes. The other day my mother said she was old enough now to fetch the water for the wash. But I go with her because she is still scared of the soldiers when she goes out alone.

In my house all the children sleep in the same room, except for Nizar, who sleeps in my parents' room because he is only two. I share my mattress with Khader and Wafa, who are younger than I am. Majda sleeps with Manaal next to the window, and Mohammed, who is ten, has his mattress near the door.

My parents have a room with a big bed and a big white wardrobe. I love to get dressed in their room because I can try on my clothes in front of my mother's mirror.

My mother is the most beautiful woman I know. Like your mother, she has a name that means something: it is "victory," or *Intissar* in Arabic. The best day this year was Mother's Day. I made cakes with Majda, and we gave her lots of presents: a nightgown, a poster, and nail polish—I picked it out. My father bought her a cake pan, and gave a pretty pair of shoes to his mother. My brothers and sisters and I sang and danced for them. I also like it when we celebrate birthdays, or when friends come to dinner. Soon we will go to my cousin's wedding.

We play a lot at the house, especially since we no longer go to school. At night when we are bored, if my father is not watching TV, he plays with us and has us sing. Manaal prefers to recite poetry while I know the most beautiful, patriotic Palestinian songs. I try to teach them to my little brothers, but the next day they have forgotten everything. So instead they dance and clap their hands.

For eight and a half months our schools have been closed by the Israeli authorities. We had to give back all our books. In the beginning I was happy. Now I am bored. I am tired of playing hopscotch and jumping rope. So I spend more time going to meetings of Palestinian women here in Dheisheh. One day they asked me to recite a poem for the celebration for the University of Birzeit*. My teacher thought I was "terrific." That made me very happy because I never think I am "terrific."

At the last meeting, the women told me that

school would soon begin again. That's good because now I realize how important it is to learn. School teaches me about justice and love for others and for my country. I don't want to be ignorant. I don't want my countrymen to be illiterate.

What do you think of school? Is your school closed too? I would like to know what games you like and if you still play them.

Mervet

September 14, 1988

◄O►

Four weeks before elections to the Israeli parliament, the Knesset (which means "Assembly" in Hebrew), the commission that is charged with ensuring democratic elections prohibits Rabbi Meir Kahane's "Kach" party from participating. "The ideology of this party threatens the democratic character of Israel," the commission states.

The militant members of Kach, called the "Yellow Shirts," promote political stands that are racist and exclusionary, notably the expulsion of all Arabs, the banning of all unpatriotic Hebrew newspapers, and the arrest of all Israelis—in particular, journalists—"who are Arab-lovers."

In addition, Kach wants to replace Israeli civil law with laws based on religious principles that are more than three thousand years old.

The same week, in Algeria, after three days of riots, a popular uprising is brutally crushed by government forces. Two hundred fifty demonstrators are killed. The Israeli right wing proposes to the army that it use the same kind of force to suppress the Palestinian revolt. This proposal is not even considered by the security forces, who, nevertheless, do impose curfews in the areas where the demonstrations are the most violent.

Jerusalem
14 September 1988

Mervet,
   Here school began two weeks ago. Only one more
year till high school! I hope it will go by quickly.
It is true that in elementary school classes are easier
and the teachers are less strict. There is at least
one thing I won't miss next year, and that's drills in
the shelters. Our teachers teach us how to protect
ourselves from bombs when there is an alert. You
have to leave the classroom quickly and calmly and
walk squeezed together close to the wall to the cellar.
We have to stay there closed up for a quarter hour
in total blackness. There isn't enough air, and
sometimes I get really jittery.
   I don't know if you agree with me or not, but I
think war is only amusing when it is a game.
Yesterday, Ayal taught me to play "Missiles" on his
computer. He let me use it because I agreed to
take Tapi, the dog, for a walk. Tapi was his birthday
present. Since he's supposed to take care of him,
he shares him more easily than his Atari! Dad got
him the computer for his Bar Mitzvah*. In our
religion, when a boy is [thirteen] he has to make a
blessing in the synagogue and wear a very long
bracelet around his forearm.
   The same custom exists for girls and it is called
"Bat Mitzvah*," but there is no ceremony in the
synagogue*†. Next year, it will be my turn. I will get

†Girls sometimes celebrate their Bat Mitzvah when they turn twelve.

(19)

lots of presents. I have already asked my father for a drum. I'm scared though that I will have to let all my relatives and all these friends I hardly know hug and kiss me.

About games, I no longer roller-skate. My skates are too small. I would rather go to the swimming pool with Ayala, my best friend, or go shopping. I also like video games a lot. At home, like you, I take care of my younger sisters. In the summer the three of us play together in the garden. We have a big garden with fruit trees and cactus. My father takes care of it. I water sometimes. In the summer I water myself to cool off.

I have to go now. My mother is waiting to take me to buy my school books. If I don't answer your next letter right away, don't worry. I might have too much homework. I hope you will start school again soon. Tell the other Arabs not to throw stones at Israeli cars or at our soldiers. Then maybe the soldiers will change their minds.

Your friend,
Galit

P.S. By the way, what do you think of the Israelis?

October 30, 1988

―◄○►―

The legislative elections will be held in three days. Who will win? The right wing, with its hard-line positions, or the left, which has a more conciliatory attitude toward the Palestinian problem? The campaign is very close, and the increasing incidents in the occupied territories risk tipping the balance in one direction or the other.

In a Palestinian attack against a bus at the end of the day in Jericho, an Israeli mother and her three children are burned alive. Public opinion is one of profound shock. The Jericho region is closed off to journalists.

Dheisheh
30 October 1988

Dear Galit,
　You're right when you say that war is better when it's only a game.
　In Dheisheh our favorite game is called "the Arabs and the soldiers," the only game I still play once in a while. We split up into two teams. The boys are the soldiers, and the girls and the little ones are the Arabs. The Arabs pretend to be demonstrators and the soldiers hit us. The Arabs run to hide where they can and some are caught. Some collapse because they pretend to be wounded. When I play this game with Mohammed, my [other] brothers, and

the children in the neighborhood, I am always the
doctor. I run to take care of the wounded with old
rags and a bottle of water. Obviously, it is always
the Arabs who win in the end. . . .

But I also know about the real demonstrations.
They happen often in Dheisheh. Everyone throws
stones. The young people make fun of the soldiers,
scream, and scrawl graffiti such as "With our soul
and our blood we will avenge our martyrs." As soon
as the soldiers come near, we have to escape as
quickly as possible. I'm afraid that Mohammed will
be arrested one day; he always has pockets full of
stones. You asked me what I think of the Israelis. For
me, they are like other people. They are free and
they have things we don't have.

I don't like the Jews because they took our country
and they mistreat Arabs. But I don't know any
Israelis other than the soldiers.

Here, no one will stop throwing stones as long as
there are soldiers. Especially since the intifada.
They make our lives difficult with arrests, wounded
people, and deaths. They throw tear gas, shoot
bullets, and destroy our homes.

Not ours, luckily. They have only blown up our
hot-water heater. Even so, our family is always
worried.

I have an uncle who has lived in hiding since his
wedding day. He sometimes comes back secretly
to see his wife, and no one else can see him. My
mother's other brother and my grandfather are
in prison in Hebron*.

My grandmother complains that even though she has four sons, she lives alone. By chance our house is right next door to hers. I often go with Manaal to help her with her housekeeping. She likes to tell us lots of stories about the beautiful life they had in Palestine* before 1948. Next time I will write you about our history as refugees. Grandmother, who is seventy-five years old, never gives up hope. She always says: "I am ready to lose my own children if it means that their children regain their nation."

How do you see the intifada in Jerusalem?

You have a very pretty smile in the picture you sent me.

Mervet

December 14, 1988

◄○►

*Five days ago, the Palestinians peacefully celebrated the first
anniversary of the intifada. According to the United Nations
Relief and Works Agency (UNRWA)*, the casualty toll is high.
Out of twenty-four thousand Palestinians wounded in the West
Bank territories and twelve thousand in Gaza, 58 percent are
less than fifteen years old. The Arabs intentionally send children
out on the front lines of battle for political reasons.*

*But it was yesterday that a historic event occurred, giving
hope to those supporting peace: in front of the United Nations
General Assembly, Yassir Arafat, for the first time, recognized
the right of Israel to live in peace and security and declared
that the Palestinians would totally give up terrorism. He challenged the Israelis: "Come, come, make the peace of the brave."*

*Up until that time, the Palestinians had never recognized
the 1947 United Nations resolution declaring the establishment
of a Jewish and an Arab state. The residents of the occupied
territories danced in the streets. But Arafat was not speaking
for all Palestinians. Subsequent massacres would show that
many militant Palestinians had no intention of giving up
terrorism against Israel.*

Jerusalem
14 December 1988

Dear Mervet,

Why do you say you hate Israelis when the only Israelis you know are the soldiers? You are the one who said you don't hate anyone. . . .

I agree that you should also have a country, but do you know that many Arabs want to push us, the Jews, into the sea? No Israeli can support something as horrible as that. Why are the Arabs and the Jews always at war? Why do Arab parents let their children throw stones at our cars? The intifada is a war without weapons, but who knows how it will end?

Before she died, my grandmother in Haifa often told me about the real war. She was very old and sick, but she remembered it as if it were yesterday. Mamy was an Ashkenazi* Jew from Czechoslovakia. She was sixteen when the Germans put her and her family in a concentration camp*. My father wasn't born yet. Those monsters gave each person ten minutes to do their washing. One day she took too long and another Jew in the camp reported her. She was hit fifty times with a whip. As a result, one of her vertebrae was out of alignment and she suffered from back pain all her life. But she said it was a miracle that she survived. At first her stories gave me nightmares. I tried to draw them, but I wasn't very successful.

My father draws them better than anyone else in

the family. He always uses a black marker on white
paper. Nothing else. He even made a series of little
drawings like a comic strip. The first drawing is a
group of prisoners behind barbed wire and some
birds on the horizon. In the second, the prisoners
sink into a hole. In the last, there is only the hole,
no prisoners, and the birds are flying right above.

I rummage around to look at them because none
of his drawings are framed. Daddy is also an artist.
He draws, he sculpts, and he does all the maintenance
work in the house and garden. He barely finished
building an aquarium and now he wants to make the
house bigger.

We are sort of squeezed in the house. My parents
sleep in the living room and they put Irit and Yael
in the little room next to the kitchen. My bed and
Ayal's are on the landing and Tally sleeps just
under us. We don't complain. It's better to have a
big family—don't you think so? Write soon.

Galit

January 1, 1989

◄O►

The first of January is the birthday of the creation of Fatah.
But it's not a festive occasion. Under the occupation, this event,
like other celebrations and religious holidays, has become a
day of conflict with the army. Nine wounded Palestinians are
hospitalized before nightfall. At night, thirteen Palestinians,
including Ibraham Faraj, a twenty-five-year-old neighbor of
Mervet's, are deported from the occupied territories into Lebanon.*

Dheisheh
1 January 1989

My dear Galit,

I am so happy: they reopened our school and my
grandfather will be released from prison this year!
He was thrown in jail because they discovered
explosives buried in our garden three years ago.

I have a ton of homework these days because we
have to catch up all the time we lost these last few
months. Every night we are buried in our books. The
house has never been so quiet.

I promised to tell you the story of my family. My
grandparents lived in a village near Hebron. They
told me that they napped on the lawn, grew their
own vegetables, and made their own clothes. The
village was called Zakariya, but it doesn't exist

anymore. In 1948 the Palestinians had to leave their land because they were driven out by the Jews†. Dheisheh was a barren hillside and they settled there with other refugees. In the beginning they didn't have a house or water or shelter. UNRWA gave them tents to sleep in. When it rained the streets were flooded and filled with mud. In the winter the babies screamed from the cold, and the wind sometimes carried away the tents. My grandmother had to walk more than a mile to get firewood and water. The water container had to last a week for the whole family. They cooked the food they received from UNRWA on a campfire because that was all they had. The poorest families in Dheisheh still get food from the UN.

After 1950 they started to build small houses. They had one room for households of five or less and two rooms for bigger families. After fifteen years my parents were able to build a big three-room house with a kitchen, running water, and electricity.

My favorite place in the house is the terrace. From there, there is a nice view of Dheisheh and the road. I can also see when the soldiers are coming.

You haven't written me about what Jerusalem is like.

In your last letter there is a word I didn't understand. It was "Ashkenazi."

Mervet

---

†Mervet's grandparents cannot have been driven out of their village by Jews, because the Jews did not live in Hebron at that time. Perhaps it was the British or the Jordanian authorities, who were in the process of gaining control of Hebron from the British.

January 30, 1989

◄○►

Faisal al-Husseini was freed after six months of administrative detention*. Fifty years old, he lives in the Arab section of Jerusalem. He is the son of the legendary Abdel-Kader al-Husseini, commander in chief of the Palestinian forces at the beginning of the Israeli-Palestinian war of 1947, who was killed in combat in April 1948. Faisal "the Moderate" is the most important individual in the occupied territories. Later, he would be a leader in the peace negotiations with Israel.

In the meantime the intifada has intensified: in Bethlehem, Palestinians threw stones at several military vehicles and cars owned by settlers, while in Gaza, five hundred youths organized a march waving Palestinian flags.

According to representative A. Rubinstein, about twenty-nine thousand Palestinians have been arrested since the beginning of the uprising; however, this does not include the eight thousand indicted leaders and four thousand found guilty.

Jerusalem
30 January 1989

Dear Mervet,
    "Ashkenazi" means to be from Poland, Russia, Romania, Germany, or Czechoslovakia like my grandmother in Haifa. It is mainly the Jews from Europe. Not all the Jews who live in Israel were born here. For two thousand years our people have

lived in different countries. Before Israel, in many countries, we were hated and we were chased out simply because we were Jewish.

There is another very big community of Jews known as Sephardic Jews [Jews of ancient Spanish origin], like my grandparents on my mother's side. They come from Morocco. When an Israeli is born in an Arab country, he is Sephardic. I am neither. I am a "Sabra*" because I was born here.

Today there are Jews on every continent in the world. They have different names depending on where they come from. One day, at the bus stop, I saw Ethiopian Jews who are black. They are called "Falashas*." When they decide to live in Israel, the government helps them to make a life here and to learn Hebrew. My grandmother Ninette, from Morocco, told me that it isn't easy to be a new immigrant* here.

When they arrived in Israel, they began their lives over with nothing. They sometimes tell me about how they had to find a house and a job when they knew no one. I often spend the weekend with them. When Grandma works I help her in the store. I love to wrap gifts. It's a store that sells souvenirs and embroidery on Jaffa Road in the center of the city. The embroidery is very beautiful. In addition to the linens and bags, she also sells hand-embroidered dresses. The patterns are very similar to your Arab dresses.

The women who know how to do this embroidery are old Jews from Yemen. I have visited two of them who live in one small room. Grandma Ninette sent me one day to bring them some new work. They are really old and poor. I gave them my package, but we didn't speak. I am so shy with older people that I didn't dare ask them their stories and how old they were when they learned to do this complicated embroidery. It seems that when they die, no one in Israel will know how to embroider the way they do.

Grandma has already teased me that it surely won't be me who will replace them.

Do you know how to embroider? I am terrible. I do a little better with knitting. Grandma is teaching me. Besides, I like it. I have started a dark green scarf for my father. I really want it to come out well. When my stitches are uneven, I undo them and I redo them. I bet my grandmother a movie ticket that I would finish before next winter!

In any case, what I like best is fashion and elegant clothes. When I grow up, I would like to be a designer or a model. Actually I can't decide between lots of things. I could also be a sketch artist because I love that.

When I have a bad dream or when I am sad, I take a pencil and, like Daddy, I draw. I try to put all my sadness in my drawings. Afterward I feel much better. Better than when my best friend comforts me. Last Saturday I was thinking about my grandmother in Haifa. So I drew a crying woman. Daddy told me I was getting much better.

I also draw when I am happy, but then I make

collages with happier things: flowers, fish, clouds, or beautiful rainbows.

I also like to watch TV. And you? Do you watch *Dynasty*?

By chance I saw a show on the refugee camps. The people slept on the ground. I have slept on the ground twice in my life when my father was building the second floor on our house. I was afraid that the walls were going to fall down on top of me. I asked my mother how you manage, and she said it was a question of customs and of habit.

I won't hide from you that, personally, I would be bored if I lived there. I prefer to live in the city because there are stores, movies, and video arcades. My favorite part of Jerusalem is the Old City*. But I guess there are things in your place that I know nothing about. In the beginning, for example, I imagined that you didn't even have a kitchen in your house. Do you have stores? Don't forget to tell me what your favorite TV show is.

Your friend,
Galit

February 22, 1989
—◄o►—

After four Arab-Israeli wars since 1948, Egypt is the only Arab country to have signed a peace treaty with Israel. Egypt is now making an effort to help the other Arab countries, and especially the Palestinians, make peace with Israel. In Cairo, the capital of Egypt, a first significant step has been taken in this direction: for the first time, the Soviet Union has joined the United States to open a discussion between the Palestinians and the Israelis. Eduard Shevardnadze, the Soviet minister of foreign affairs, met his Israeli counterpart, Moshe Arens, and the head of the PLO, Yassir Arafat. Shevardnadze had no success. Despite increasing international pressure, the two camps refuse to sit down at the negotiating table.

Dheisheh
22 February 1989

Dear Galit,

Your letter made me happy. I know you better now. What you write me changes my thinking a little.

You see, I would like to live with you, and you're especially lucky not to live a life as hard as ours.

There are more and more arrests, and the curfew now lasts several days in a row. The soldiers arrest boys for nothing. They want to prevent the intifada. So the men who distribute political pamphlets go out in secret at night. They all wear a "kaffiyeh*" over their faces so no one will know who they are. But there isn't just the police to watch out for. We also have traitors*, like in all wars.

One time you wrote me that I was wrong to hate the Israelis. I wouldn't say that anymore because, for example, you are an Israeli and we get along. But I swear to you that the soldiers here are horrible. They treat us badly and beat us like donkeys. One day, in the school courtyard, a little boy lost his eye when he was hit with a rubber bullet. I fainted. I will never be able to forget this.

Last night we took in a wounded man. From the window I saw the *chababs** arrive. They were carrying a body and they came to ask us for first aid. The man was covered with blood because he had been shot in the stomach. My father couldn't do much. He works at the hospital, but he isn't a doctor. He tried anyway to find the wound. Soldiers rang the doorbell, and my mother went outside and said there was no one in the house. Once they left, she ran next door to use the phone. Fifteen minutes later a car came and took the wounded man to the hospital. This afternoon we heard he was operated on and is out of danger. The whole family was relieved to hear the good news.

Before, the young people in the camp weren't as bored, because there was more to do. There were tennis courts, a basketball court, and a youth club. It's been years since the military closed all of them because our camp is well-known for its political activism. In addition to poor people, we also have lots of prisoners because the residents have remained very militant here.

Since the intifada, they built a very high barricade to stop us from throwing stones on the cars in the road. The army has closed all the entrances to the camp except for one. It is right near our school, but it's not the one closest to our house. I have to walk twice as far. When there are heavy rains, like we've had recently, the big hill that leads to the house is transformed into a mud slide.

Another big problem at Dheisheh is the sewers. The camp is so overpopulated that the dirty water overflows and runs in the gutter all day long.

You asked me if we have stores. Yes, but not many. Only about ten. Here the stores are only open in the morning. When there is a general strike* in support of the intifada, they stay shut all day long. At Dheisheh we buy vegetables and food. If we need shoes or clothes, Daddy brings them back from Bethlehem. Abou-Roulouz's grocery store is at the bottom of our street. When I was younger, I went to play hide-and-seek in front of his store every day after school. Abou-Roulouz often scolded us because we made too much noise. He is an old man who is seventy years old. He likes children, but like all old people, he gets annoyed if he is disturbed. To calm us down, he would tell us stories about how life used to be in Palestine.

He knows everyone in the camp and where each family comes from. He played guessing games with

us. He asked each of us our last names and then said,
"You come from Zakariya. Your grandfather was
born in Beit Itab and your grandmother in Albourej."
My sister Manaal, who was only six, thought he
was a magician.

It's like another life when you're little. When I
was five I thought we lived in Zakariya. I was afraid
of the soldiers, and, I admit, I was more afraid than
Manaal. I didn't dare go out into the street. Now
I give stones to the *chababs,* and the army is just part
of normal life. I almost never play anymore. I
spend my time reading or I plant flowers. Knitting
is not at all my thing. You are surely better at it
than I am. There is one thing I want to learn how
to do—to make a Palestinian bracelet. Tomorrow
I am going to my neighbor Fatia, who is fifteen. She
has promised to teach me how to weave it with
the three colors of our flag. If it is not too hard, I
will be able to make at least three; that way all my
sisters can have one. I already have a bracelet like
this, but when I go to school, I am always careful
to hide it under my smock sleeve. I don't want the
soldiers to see it. It is forbidden like the flags that
the boys tie onto the electrical wires.

I don't watch much television. Only once in a
while. My father, who speaks Hebrew, watches the
news on Israeli TV almost every day.

I sometimes watch the Arab soap opera, but I
couldn't tell you the story because I miss at least
half the shows. The only show I like is the *Tom and
Jerry* cartoons. Their games and their funny actions

make me laugh. It's funny to see that, for once, a cat and mouse get along.

I hope I haven't bored you with my long letter.

Do you know any Arabs in Jerusalem? You are so lucky to be able to live in Jerusalem.

I hope none of your cousins is doing military service in our camp. Tell me the truth, please.

Mervet

March 14, 1989

━◀○▶━

On the beach in Taba, at the head of the Gulf of Aqaba in the Sinai, a Tsahal* officer carefully folds the blue-and-white Israeli flag. An Egyptian officer, in a white uniform, raises the flag of his country.

Taba, a tiny enclave on the Red Sea, which the two countries have fought over for years, has returned to Egypt. The last of the disputes between the two former enemies has been amicably resolved.

This symbolic act of peace has not stopped the daily violence: a Palestinian girls' school organized a demonstration during which an Israeli bank was bombarded with rocks and traffic was stopped with trash cans and paving stones. A group of settlers from the group "Committee for Safe Travel," affiliated with Kach, vandalized the market in Hebron, turning over tables, breaking windows, destroying merchandise, and shooting guns.

Jerusalem
14 March 1989

My dear Mervet,

Your letter didn't bore me at all. To the contrary, I am very happy because I never would have imagined your life the way you described it. Can you believe it? We are fifteen minutes away from each other, and it's as if we were on two distant planets.

The worst is, you and I are so insignificant. I often ask myself why the Arabs and the Jews are always at war. I know that a long time ago the Arabs invaded our land and then we took it back. Now everyone wants the land.

I asked my father about the army. No one in the family is doing his *milouim** in the occupied territories. By the way, can you explain to me how the curfew works for you?

I may be lucky to live in Jerusalem, but, believe me, it's not paradise either. It's true that Jerusalem is a beautiful city with a magnificent view, museums, and plenty of stores, but you feel the war here too. Now, in the Old City, people are being stabbed. I heard that, there, Arab women help the men kill Israelis. I learned that a lot of soldiers have been killed. If only the Arabs and the Jews would stop fighting. For months I haven't dared go into the Old City. My parents have strictly forbidden it.

It is awful not to be free. I used to go to the "Kotel*" almost every week. You can put a message with a prayer that means a lot to you between the stones in the wall. If God agrees, your hope will become reality. Of course, you have to be patient! I have put in dozens of wishes that Daddy would stop smoking, but it hasn't worked! My grandfather Yaakov, the one from Morocco, sometimes goes to pray at the wall because it brings good luck. I give him my wishes. He is the only one in the family who can do errands in the Old City. He often brings us fruit and vegetables. Mom and Grandma are always afraid something awful will happen to him. Grandpa always calms them down because he says he knows the Arabs. He lived with them in Morocco. He also speaks Arabic, and so, if something happened, he could speak to them to defend himself.

I don't know many Arabs other than our gardener and a woman who sells fruit in our neighborhood. The only other ones are people I meet in Daddy's factory.

Before the intifada, my father had an Arab friend who worked at the factory with him. He would come to say hello to us, and sometimes we went to visit his family on Saturdays. They lived on a farm with an orchard, where they raised all kinds of animals: chickens, rabbits, goats. When his children showed me the farm it was really funny. We smiled a lot and talked with our hands. Now the place where they live has become too dangerous. We would have stones thrown at our car. It's too bad that we can never see them again. They were always so nice to us. I remember how they used to serve us coffee in tiny cups like dollhouse cups. You don't drink the same coffee that we do. Israeli coffee is weaker and is served in big cups. In our house we put coffee powder in hot water, while you boil the two together, right?

I went to a restaurant in Haifa with my father once. The waiter was a young Arab boy, and he was so nice! Not like the ones who throw stones or bottle bombs. Do you know that when the police stop them, they say they haven't done anything.

The TV news is on and I'm going to turn off the TV because I can't stand hearing every day about the dead, the wounded, and the suffering.

Besides Ayala is coming soon. She is my best friend. Since my parents are going out tonight, she is coming to help me take care of Irit and Yael. Ayala is the sweetest person in my class. We have known each other since kindergarten. Outside of school we walk in town, and in the summer, we go to the swimming pool together. When I told her our story she understood. The others don't know that I am writing to you. Who knows, maybe they would be jealous or they would pretend not to believe me just to annoy me. They annoy me so much that I don't care if they never know that I have an Arab friend.

I wanted to tell you about my neighborhood. I already told you that I live on Bethlehem Road. It's the old road that leads to Bethlehem, right near you. We have very nice neighbors and here everyone helps each other. When my father has a migraine, for example, they are happy to give us aspirin. If I see an old lady walking by with her groceries, I immediately offer to help her. The only one who bugs me is our grocer. Yours sounds like a nice old grandfather, while ours always makes me mad. I hate his jokes that no one thinks are funny. Plus, I've noticed that he cheats his customers. If I complain about it he'll tell me I'm stupid and that I don't understand anything. Anyway, as my grandmother says, "It takes all kinds to make a world." My grandmother Ninette also lives in Baka. It is very handy because I only have a five-minute walk to see her.

I'm going tomorrow afternoon. She promised to help me with a costume for Purim* next Sunday.

It's my favorite Jewish holiday. That day we eat cookies called hamantaschen, or "Haman's ear." In the legend, Haman was a mean man in Persia who tried to hurt the Jews. It's a kind of vengeance to say now that we are eating his ear. What customs do you have? I like Purim because we put on costumes. I also use disguises when we play. In the summer, in our garden, Irit, Yael, and I play a game we call "the royal court." Irit and Yael dress up like princesses and I am the queen. I make a bun with my hair and I use a scarf as a crown. When we do this I think maybe I will be an actress someday. I hear the doorbell.

Write soon, Mervet.
Galit

P.S. Don't forget to write me about what you want to be when you grow up.

May 15, 1989

Yesterday Israel celebrated the forty-first anniversary of its independence. It was a bittersweet celebration because the country hasn't known a day of peace in all those years. Is the country destined to live in war? To suffer at the hands of the Arabs and to make the neighboring Arabs suffer?

In the Gaza Strip, the acts of violence increase and the number of victims rises. Two Israeli soldiers who were hitchhiking were kidnapped and then assassinated by Palestinian extremists. Only one body was found. Anti-Arab incidents exploded in the south of Israel and the crowd attacked Palestinian workers who had come to Israel to work. The Israeli demonstrators chanted: "Death to Arabs!" The Arabs chant violent anti-Israeli slogans when they demonstrate.

But if there are a thousand reasons to be pessimistic, a new hope was born today. In Jerusalem, the government ratified a peace plan that might be successful where the others have failed. This plan proposes a solution to the Palestinian problem and peace with Arab countries. But not all the ministers agree. They are especially opposed to giving autonomy to the occupied territories, fearful that this will lead to the creation of a Palestinian state.

Dheisheh
15 May 1989

Dear Galit,

Unfortunately I couldn't write you sooner.
Between taking care of my little brothers and my
homework, I don't have much time. Mommy will
soon have the baby. I have to help as much as I
can. I was thirteen years old on April 24. Majda does
the housework. I take care of the cooking and put
Khader and Nizar to bed. They are the same age as
your sisters. Luckily, I don't have to baby-sit the
way you sit for Irit and Yael because we are never
alone in the house.

We spend evenings together as a family.
Sometimes we have company. My uncle Jawdat,
who is a journalist in Bethlehem, often comes with
friends who want to see Dheisheh. It always makes
me happy when strangers come to see us. I wish I
spoke better English so I could speak with them
and show them that I am an educated young woman.

On these occasions, Mommy always makes the
best meals. Stuffed grape leaves and chicken and
rice. The children listen to the adult conversations.

My brother Mohammed is the one who argues
politics best of all. Obviously, all our conversations
center on Palestine. The old ones tell about how we
were forced out and the young ones swear that
with the intifada, we will chase Israel off our land.
Mohammed asks the visitors if they are Americans.
Often they say yes. So he asks, "Do you like us?" and

they say, "Yes." So then he tells them, "If you like us, why do you give the Israelis arms, tanks, and tear gas to fight us?" They don't know what to answer, and I am very proud of him.

After dinner my father often asks me to sing. He says I have the best voice of all the children. Maybe he is right. I love to sing. I like ordinary songs like those of Feirouz or Julia Butros, two Lebanese singers. But the older I get, I find patriotic songs much more beautiful.

Here's one:

> *You, the children of Palestine,*
> *You who are near*
> *You who are far,*
> *Bring your tears*
> *Come to save this country.*
>
> *Children of Palestine*
> *Never forget*
> *The perfume of your land.*
>
> *Palestine, light which*
> *Will never be extinguished by slander.*
> *The intifada will rebuild*
> *Our destroyed houses.*
>
> *Martyrs or wounded ones,*
> *Your blood will be avenged.*
> *Dignity for all will be returned*
> *When Palestine is delivered.*

When I sing, my heart beats faster and I get the shivers. Before the intifada, my father encouraged me to sing at weddings. Now, he says, our celebrations have become like funerals because we are in mourning for our *chahids**. Before there were orchestras at every wedding. People paraded to fetch the bride. We made big meals; we spent whole days singing, dancing, and laughing. This year when my cousin was married, there was only one car to get the bride and no musicians.

The curfews can last hours or whole days, maybe even a week. We can't go out or open the doors or the windows. Now, with the intifada, only people with jobs can leave the camp in the morning.

My father, for example, has a special card that he shows at the roadblock and the soldiers let him go.

I remember when I was little and I thought we lived in Zakariya, there were days when my father wouldn't let me out to play. I didn't understand and I would ask him questions. He answered that it was the curfew, but I didn't understand what that was. The soldiers declare a curfew every time there is a demonstration or a Jewish holiday. Also when American politicians come to Israel.

A few months ago I had the bad luck to run into the army when there was a curfew. When our schools were closed I was a volunteer for the committee of Palestinian women. I went there every morning and helped the children to learn to read and write. We also gave out food, books, and notebooks. It cost five shekels* per child, but we never refused any children who didn't have money.

That day, my mother had forbidden me from leaving the house, but I didn't listen to her. That afternoon, with the other women of the committee, we wanted to visit the family of Nasser, one of our martyrs. It had been just one year since his death. On the way we ran into some soldiers who made us turn around.

We waited a little until the *chababs* told us that the soldiers had left. We were almost at the door of Nasser's house, near my street, when we ran into them again. They insulted and threatened us: "We already stopped you. Why are you back out? If we see you again you will be imprisoned."

My worst nightmare is that I will be a martyr or be imprisoned. Yesterday, I was in Abou-Roulouz's grocery store and I hid in the store for fifteen minutes, waiting for the soldiers to leave. I swear that afterward I felt like I had escaped from prison.

I told you that I'm not afraid, but I admit I preferred to wait because you never know with the soldiers if they will decide to start shooting. Have you heard of Nahalin? It is a village near Hebron where, last month, they killed five people and wounded thirty more. They wanted to come into the village and they shot at anything—they even killed sheep.

You asked me what I want to do later. My goal in life is to go to the university and to become a doctor. I want to help sick people regardless of race or religion. My people are very poor and our women suffer a lot when they give birth. There are families in Dheisheh who don't have enough money to pay for medicine or for a doctor. I want to be a light for them, a gentle hand on their wounds. I would build a hospital for everyone. Even if I get married, I would still be a doctor. I would have a big house and an import-export business to distribute clothes to the poor. I would also have a playground and a sports club and an immense park in Dheisheh. I want our camp to be the most beautiful of all the camps. I want my children to have all they need. I will teach them literature and good manners. I also want to visit Jordan. I dream about it. I'm sure it is a thousand times more beautiful than it is on television.

I know that in Israeli schools you learn Arabic. Do you like your Arabic teacher?

This week is the holiday of "Id and Fitr*." This holiday comes the week after Ramadan*, which is the required fast for all Muslims. This year it began on April 13. For forty days I can't eat or drink between four in the morning and seven in the evening. When the sun sets, the "muezzin*" makes the call to prayer: *Allahou akbar*, and it is only then that I can eat. In my family only Khader and Nizar don't fast for Ramadan because they are still too young.

Our biggest holiday is the Feast of the Sacrifice*, which comes three months after the end of Ramadan. My mother will give birth before then. But I don't think we will have a big celebration because my grandfather is still in prison. I hope this will be the last sad holiday in my whole life.

I also hope we will get to meet each other soon.

Your friend,
Mervet

May 31, 1989

━◄○►━

*The settlers—nationalist Israelis who live in the occupied terri-
tories, which they want to annex—push the government to
stiffen the repression of the Palestinians. "If you don't," they
add, "we will do it ourselves."*

*Two days ago an armed leader of the settlers attacked an
Arab village, killing a sixteen-year-old girl. "An example of
reprisal," they said.*

*In Ariel, the biggest Jewish settlement in the occupied territor-
ies, an anti-Arab measure has been implemented. Since this
morning, free access by Palestinians has been forbidden. Those
who have jobs in the neighborhood can enter, but they will
have to wear a white badge declaring them to be "foreign
workers." This discriminatory act reminds some Holocaust*
survivors of the "yellow star"—the yellow star of David that
the Nazis required all Jews to wear on their sleeves to prevent
them from working, shopping, or attending school, and to mark
them for transport to the concentration camps, where millions
died—and a disagreement has exploded among Israelis. But
the settlers do not want to hear about it and reject all accusations
of racism, promising to increase the number of "security measures" like this one.*

Jerusalem
31 May 1989

Dear Mervet,

> *In the garden I sit*
> *Near my grandmother,*
> *Who like today tells and retells what*
> *this country was a long time ago.*
>
> *A blue and white flag*
> *Like today,*
> *Which tomorrow will also be blue and white,*
> *The same as the sand and sea.*

This is a poem about Israel that I sang in school
when I was little. I remember the tune very well.
It is simple and very pretty. So I taught it to Irit and
Yael. When it comes to singing, I don't know why,
but I am not like you. The older I get, the less this
kind of song amuses me. I prefer groups like U2
or the New Kids. Do you know them? I listen to them
every Saturday on the radio. There are also rock
songs in Hebrew. I can sing those better than the
English songs, because the English they teach us
in school is nothing like the English in rock music.
    I wanted to tell you about a book I finished
reading today, which really made me dream. The
story is about a sheepherder who, like Zorro, can see
everything but can't be seen. He defends his
friends against the mean boys in the neighborhood.

He always wears a monkey fur. He can disappear
when he wants, and the police can never catch him.
If we could be like him, the soldiers would never
notice you, and I could come and visit you every
week.

Today is our Shabbat*, our day of rest. My parents
went to Haifa. I spent the whole afternoon in the
garden with Irit and Yael. Like always, I dressed up
as a queen and they were princesses. They danced
and sang for me. Our throne is the big swing in the
garden and Tapi, our dog, is the horse. We
playacted for hours. I didn't notice the time going
by, and I can't even tell you about the mess in the
house. There were clothes everywhere, because we
make our hairstyles and our costumes with old
fabrics of my mother's. I have to clean up right away
before they come home. That way Mom won't be
mad at me.

It's done! It's not perfect, but that's okay. Tonight
it will be a mess again when we clean the aquarium.
I haven't told you yet about our fish. In the beginning
there were five. Since then, one died because he
was eaten. I don't understand it, but there are some
fish that eat others. Daddy calls them "killers." So
we have to isolate them, especially when the little fish
are first born. Luckily, they multiply all the time.
When a female fish gets pregnant, her stomach gets
all round like women's do. So then we put her in
a separate jar, all alone until her babies are born.
Then we wait at least one month before we let
them swim with the big fish.

Daddy built the aquarium. He decorated it with plants, shells, and different-size stones. He put in a special thing so the fish can breathe and lighting and a thermometer. I feed the fish twice a day. Cleaning the aquarium is Daddy's job. I help him take the fish out of the water. Then we take out all the gear, dump the old water, and clean the interior with a rag. Once the cleaning is done, we change the water and put each thing back one at a time. It takes forever. I can tell you that Tally has the time to go to the movies and come back.

I don't know anything about Ramadan. For us, when the sun sets it has a different meaning. Like today, for example, in a few minutes Shabbat will be over. Then, people can return to work or drive a car. But not everyone follows the old rules. There are Jewish families like mine who are more liberal. I don't agree with the old-fashioned Hasidim* who want to stop the others from driving or going to the movies on Saturday. Luckily they don't run the government or we would be living in an antique society.

I don't have an Arabic teacher at school. Arabic is an option only next year. I have already thought about it. I asked my mother if she would agree, but she prefers that I take French. She says it will be much more useful for my career when I grow up.

The other day I went to my father's factory. I go often. When I came back from the bathrooms, I passed a group of Arab women talking in the hall. When I passed them they stopped talking, and

they stared at me strangely from head to toe. Then
I heard them laugh as though they were mocking
me. I swear they looked mean. Luckily not all Arabs
are like that. At Yerolin, there is an Arab man who
is very nice. I like to help him when he has a lot of
groceries to move. But there are others who are
apparently lazy. My father told me another story from
his factory. There is an Arab woman who speaks
Hebrew, but she refuses to do it. My father is very
honest with people. When they are working, my
father asked her to answer in Hebrew. So she made
fun of him and said, "Is it raining today?" He was
very angry. I think if they hadn't been in the factory,
he would have hit her.

Sometimes I like to go to my mother's office. I
help her make copies and then I file them in
different mailboxes. There, the people are very nice,
and there is also a movie theater on the ground
floor. I either go after school in the afternoon or
with my parents in the evening. The other day it
was the anniversary of the creation of Israel and they
showed a movie about the Holocaust. Our country
has existed since May 14, 1948. The Holocaust took
place before the existence of Israel. The Holocaust
is the history of all the suffering of the Jews, like that
of my grandmother, during the big war of 1940.

Soon I will have exams and then it will be vacation.
I will be able to spend more time in the garden
with my sisters. In the summer my mother sets up an
inflatable pool for Irit and Yael. I use it too, but
when it is too hot I prefer the real swimming pool,

which is five minutes away from us. Do you have a big garden?

During vacation I will spend several days with my uncle, who lives on the "moshav*." It's like a village, and everyone knows each other, but the houses are spread out. The residents work the land and share the harvest. It is very beautiful there, but it is boring. The parents don't let their children have any freedom. So I go to the swimming pool, where I don't have any friends. It makes me want to go right home. What I can't stand there is that the people scream all the time instead of speaking in a normal voice. I'm not used to it, and it drives me crazy.

I prefer when Daddy takes us to Haifa for the weekend. You see, my parents don't have much vacation time this year, so there is only Friday and Saturday to go to the beach. Plus we won't go every weekend because it's not that close. Sometimes, at the last minute, my parents cancel the trip. I don't think that's fair. I hate it when people don't keep their promises.

How will you spend your vacation? I wouldn't be surprised that you have to stay home since your mother is having a baby. I'm waiting to hear from you. For me, I will be able to answer quickly because after my exams I will have plenty of time to write you.

Galit

July 7, 1989

◄○►

Yesterday was marked by two tragedies. In Nablus, a ten-year-old Palestinian child was killed by Israeli soldiers. Several hours later, a twenty-five-year-old Palestinian, originally from Gaza, threw himself on a bus driver of the 405 bus line*, which links Tel Aviv with Jerusalem. Shouting "Allahou akbar!," he grabbed the steering wheel from the driver and deliberately steered the bus into a ravine. Sixteen Israeli passengers were killed and twenty-five were hurt, six of whom were seriously injured. The perpetrator of this suicide act, who was only slightly hurt, was arrested by the police. He declared, "I acted alone for vengeance."

Israeli Prime Minister Yitzhak Shamir modified the Israeli peace plan, refusing to negotiate until the intifada is stopped and encouraging Jewish settlements in the occupied territories. Israeli and Palestinian extremists have redoubled their efforts to force the collapse of the peace process with hate and blood.

Dheisheh
7 July 1989

My dear Galit,

I waited for the birth of my brother, Nabil, to write to you. Nobody other than my mother knew that it would be a boy. When she gave birth, the whole camp came to visit us with gifts. The family of the big Nabil was the first to come.

June 17, at dawn, my mother went to the hospital with my father and Mohammed. That afternoon I heard my brother come back screaming with joy: "Nabil, our Nabil is here!" Our brother has the name of the big Nabil, one of the martyrs of our camp. I have to tell you the story from the beginning.

One day the soldiers shot into a crowd of people in Dheisheh who were protesting an arrest. A fifteen-year-old boy was wounded. He wanted to escape through our garden, but he collapsed in front of the door. My mother ran to help him and accompanied him to the hospital with the neighbors. On the way to the hospital he opened his eyes. He looked at my mother and squeezed her arm. Then he died before he even got to the hospital.

Because she was six months pregnant, the whole family was very worried about her health, as she was very upset by this event. She began weaving and sewing clothes for a little boy, as if she knew in advance that she would give birth to a little Nabil. She said she knew it when the big Nabil looked right into her eyes. That's how they decided to name my brother after the young man who was killed.

We have had several martyrs in the camp since the start of the intifada. I have kept pictures of all of them. Everyone respects their families, and to honor them, we give their names to our babies. Did you know that in Palestine we have many little girls who are named Intifada?

I remember that when my mother was still at the

hospital, I heard Roufaida's mother shrieking in the hallway. I even tried to calm her, but it was impossible. Yesterday I hung the photo of Roufaida in my room, next to Ibrahim, Nasser, and Nabil. I wrote a little inscription: "the first young girl martyr of Bethlehem." I admire the martyrs, but I intend to live to liberate my country rather than die for it. Last night I dreamed that we were finally free, but the soldiers had taken Mohammed hostage.

My country is Palestine. In the bottom of my heart, I want it to exist soon and that it should be a free country with a government and good spirit, the most beautiful of all the Arab countries.

My pencil pushes me to write the things I need to tell you. Here, no one supports the occupation, the deportations, and the imprisonments. Do you understand that such a life is unbearable? In my family, like in all the families, we will never forget how the army chased my family out of Zakariya. The hatred grows every day in our hearts and we want to get revenge against Israel for our martyrs. We, the children, know that we have no future if the occupation continues. Our camp is like a big prison. So we throw stones because our only thought is to chase Israel out of our land.

Don't be mad at me for being so honest in my letters. I swear I feel no hate against you because I know you and you can understand us. Even though we have never seen each other, I would like to know your opinion. I want to know if you agree that the Palestinians should live free on their land. You might have a hard time imagining our life here, but I beg you, try to understand.

The hot weather has started. I will obviously spend the summer here, but that doesn't bother me. I hope the time will go by quickly because my grandfather will get out of prison in September, and we are waiting until he returns to circumcise* Nabil. We don't worry about vacation; it is not our custom. Here everyone dreams of a better life. For example, my mother wants to live elsewhere, outside of Dheisheh, because it is more and more crowded here. I don't totally agree with her because I was born here and I've grown up here. I like Dheisheh and I'm afraid I won't get used to a new place if we move.

We used to have a garden almost as big as yours. We grew tomatoes, string beans, and all sorts of vegetables. I planted the mint. But since my uncle got married he needed some land to build his house. Our garden is now covered with a layer of concrete. There are advantages and problems, obviously. Grandma says we escape the dust in the summer and the mud in the winter. At first I was sad, but I have started to grow my plants in empty jam tins and all the pails with holes that I found. Khader and Nizar are happy because now they can ride their bikes in the courtyard.

I am writing you from the terrace on the roof of our house. It is my favorite place. My father planted a vine and we have put up an arbor to have some

shade. In the afternoon I always come here to
study. Tomorrow we will all have lunch on the terrace
because it is Friday, our day of rest. It is six in the
evening and it is a little cooler now. I have finally
finished my homework and I am listening to
Lebanese songs on the radio. I don't know U2 or
American rock groups. I never listen to those
songs. Arab songs are more my style because they
come from us. I have a cousin who likes rock. I
will ask him for a cassette and I will listen to it and
let you know what I think.

The story of your phantom-boy is very funny. Right
now I am reading a novel that tells the adventure
of four Palestinian boys who go to work in Kuwait*.
They have to get past the border illegally, and they
pay a driver to hide them in a tanker truck. On the
way the truck stops every once in a while so they
can get some fresh air. I am at the point where they
are approaching the border. I will tell you the rest
in my next letter. I have to stop now because I hear
the call to prayer and that means it is time to give
Nabil his bottle. See you soon.

Your friend,
Mervet

September 20, 1989

◄○►

*Since the beginning of the intifada, the number of Palestinians
who have been shot or hacked to death by their comrades for
allegedly collaborating with the Israeli army has risen to more
than one hundred. This squaring of accounts is escalating.
The Palestinian leaders do not know how to stop the assassina-
tions or the collaboration.*

*On Mount Carmel, in the north of Israel, a fire set by
arsonists ravaged about three square miles of the most beautiful
forest in Israel. An anonymous phone call in Arabic said the
fire was vengeance in the name of an organization called Direct
Revenge. It took more than a week to bring the fire under
control. The Israelis are in despair. In this country where
vegetation is rare, forests are sacred. The fire is an unbearable
provocation.*

Jerusalem
20 September 1989

Mervet,
    You have probably wondered why it has taken me
so long to answer you. I will tell you the truth. It's
because I was angry. Against all the Arabs and
therefore against you too. When I heard about the
405 bus, I didn't want to write anymore. I thought
that the terrorist who turned the steering wheel

and who killed sixteen people in the ravine could be someone in your family. Can you explain what those people did that was so terrible that they deserved to die so horribly? I prefer to tell you my anger against those who have done this. It is the first time that I have had a chance to express it.

Today, coming back from Haifa with my parents, we drove on this road again. Each time that I go that way I am overwhelmed with anger and I want to cry. Now when I take the bus I am afraid of a terrorist attack. Before I get on, I look carefully to be sure there are no Arabs inside. If there are, I wait for the next bus. I hope you will understand my anger, especially since I don't hold you responsible anymore. I have thought about it. After all, I don't have to be afraid of you. You wouldn't hurt me. You are just like me.

We have been back in school for twenty days. I am now in the high school. It is a big coed school with one thousand students. I am getting ready for harder work and also more discipline because the teachers look very strict.

My mother has promised that soon I will have more freedom. I am not a little girl anymore. Soon I will have a boyfriend like Tally's. I will be able to talk to him and kiss him, and best of all, he will protect me in school and when we go out. When I introduce him to my parents, I'm sure that they will agree to let me stay out later at night. I am also waiting to get my period. Then I will really be grown up. But I think I will be scared to tell my mother. I hope it won't happen on my Bat Mitzvah!

I realize that thinking about all that will happen consoles me. I have cried enough today. Our family went to the cemetery in Haifa. It has been one year since my grandmother died. It's true that she was sick and old. But the day she died, that was the most horrible day of my life. I remember that I came home from school and my mother was crying and I understood.

Daddy, at the funeral, instead of only tearing a little piece of his sleeve, completely destroyed his shirt. He carved her tombstone and lit a candle in the synagogue, a candle that has to stay lit for a long time. Today, in the cemetery, when Daddy and the rabbi recited the prayer for my grandmother, I couldn't stop crying. I put my little stone* on the tombstone and I thought, I hate death.

You know, when I hear that someone has died, whether they are Arab or Jew, I am angry and I say to myself: "Why doesn't the world care?"

Will they ever decide to make peace? Every week I cling to that hope.

I agree that the Arabs should live in their own country. If I were prime minister, I would give a piece of the land to the Arabs. I would give half of the Negev*, half of Eilat*, and all of Ashdod*; it's not the prettiest city in Israel. I would also give a piece of the Galilee* except for Haifa, because that is my father's city, or Tiberias* and, obviously, never Jerusalem. Arabs and Jews living separately without bumping against each other. Maybe that way there would be peace. What do you think?

Galit

P.S. During vacation I thought about you because one day we drove past your camp. It was so fast that I didn't see much from the road. I hope, despite everything, that we will meet someday.

September 28, 1989

◄O►

*In Jerusalem, the trial of Abie Nathan, the peace activist, has
ended. The most famous Israeli pacifist is condemned to six
months of prison without parole for having met with the leader
of the PLO, Yassir Arafat. "As soon as I get out of prison,"
Nathan declares, "I will make contact with the enemy to talk
about peace." He will do it and will be sent back to prison.*

*In the occupied territories, the army has sealed the house
of Ali Nasman, leaving the twenty-five members of his family
homeless. Ali is accused of burning an Israeli truck. Three
other Palestinian families have been told to evacuate their
houses because they will be dynamited. This measure is to
punish three family members accused of attacking a Palestinian
collaborator.*

Dheisheh
27 and 28 September 1989

Galit,

Thank you for writing. To tell the truth I asked
myself lots of questions. I said to myself: "Her
letter was stolen, or she moved out." I even thought:
"Maybe my sad stories don't interest her anymore
and I'm annoying her with all this."

But you are right. You don't know how much
pleasure you gave me when you said we deserve a
land of our own. If the army could think like you,

maybe I would be free and living in Zakariya. The only one of us who goes there fairly often is my old uncle because he grows our olive trees for the settlers. For that reason we eat olives from Zakariya every year. They are the best olives in the world.

My grandfather is coming home tomorrow after four years in prison. Wait till he sees what has happened to the old garden where the searchers found the bombs! My uncle has finished building his house. These days the men work day and night. They want to finish the terrace in time for the celebration of his return. Daddy slaughtered two goats for Grandfather's first meal. This afternoon, on the terrace, Manaal and my little brothers and I picked some bunches of grapes.

I stopped this letter last night because I had to finish my English homework for the next day. My parents and Mohammed left early this morning for the prison in Hebron. There were two cars and a pickup truck to get my grandfather. What joy for my grandmother! Now I only have one uncle who is still in prison. Apparently he will be freed in a year. My mother also took Nabil with her. I had to stay here and help the other women make the meal. We will have lots of guests and the *chababs* will all come to greet him. Grandpa is highly respected in Dheisheh because he has always been an active supporter of the Fatah. I still remember the day he was arrested. When the investigators found the explosives that someone had hidden in the garden, they took him away. That night, they returned with the army, then beat my grandmother and broke the furniture in the house.

I hope that the day of our independence is not far off. We will be free and you will be less afraid. We all will be less afraid.

Galit, if you ask your grandparents they will tell you that the Arabs and Jews are descended from the same prophet, Ibrahim*. We are cousins. It's not good for cousins to fight together. I hope that the day when we can eat and drink together will come soon.

I hear honking outside. Grandpa is here. I have to quickly put on my Palestinian dress to welcome him. The party is beginning; it's about time!

I wish you much happiness.

Mervet

Later . . .

◄o►

Beginning with that autumn, there was a long silence between Galit and Mervet. For my part, I had not returned to Jerusalem for more than a year. I heard about them from mutual friends who visited me in Paris.

With time, our letters and our telephone calls grew further apart. But I knew that the gulf of violence and exclusion that separates the two peoples had deepened and written bloody new pages in the history of the Israeli-Palestinian conflict.

Then the Iraqi Scud missiles fell on Israel. Another war came to sharpen the hatred and undermine the peace dialogue.

Among the Palestinians, little girls were born and named Intifada, and little boys were named Saddam*, while in Israel the children learned to breathe with gas masks on their faces.

I saw Mervet and Galit the day after the Western victory against Iraq. They had grown. Their conversation had gotten tougher, and the magic of their friendship seemed to be paralyzed by the history of their peoples. But they both asked, "Is it too late to meet each other?"

Their words surprised me.

March 10, 1991

―◄○►―

On February 28, the Gulf War ended and Israel felt reassured. However, the theory that the occupied territories ensure the security of civilian Israelis now seems very shaky, since the forty-one Iraqi Scud missiles shot at the cities were aimed not only at army installations but also civilian sites. In effect, technological military advances now permit targets to be hit with such precision that the "safety zone" that the territories once represented is now only a strategic issue. As a result, a number of Israelis think it is time to revise the security requirements and consider a peace plan.

The Americans, principal allies in the international military coalition for the war and commanders of the operation, have opened a new front with the goal of establishing peace in the Middle East.

The Americans have great influence on Israel, because they give about $3 billion in annual aid, and no one can resist the diplomatic pressure from Washington. At the same time, the United States has accelerated the negotiations with the Arab countries, and with the support of the Soviet Union, has increased the pressure.

With an airplane converted into a flying office, U.S. Secretary of State James Baker commutes between Washington and the different capitals in the Middle East. Progress is slow, but the Americans are tireless. With seductive promises, offers of guarantees, and threats against those who try to undermine the peace process, James Baker, bit by bit, has organized a peace conference. It will be held in Madrid, Spain, in October 1991.

But, meanwhile, the violence continues. In Jerusalem, four Israeli women are stabbed by a Palestinian from Gaza. "It's a message for Baker," he says when he is arrested at the scene of the attack. James Baker is scheduled to arrive tomorrow in Jerusalem to encourage the Israelis and the Palestinians to enter into peace negotiations.

Jerusalem
10 March 1991

Mervet,

It is now almost two years since we have written. A lot has changed in my life and in this country since the war. I have grown up and matured.

During the war there were some very difficult moments for my family. Every night we had to be in the house before 6:00 P.M. It was our curfew, which was undoubtedly not as difficult as yours. We spent our evenings and our nights together in a sealed room*. At the first alert we had to put on gas masks because of the chemical weapons. My little sisters were terrorized by the sound of the sirens. They cried all the time.

On the TV they said that each time a missile landed on Israel, the Arabs were happy and danced on the roofs. That profoundly shocked me.

Since this horrible war I have changed my mind about the Arab-Israeli conflict. When I was little, I was more open to ideas because I did not understand the true significance of things. When we started to write I was in the "Hashomer Hatzair*" movement, which is favorable to Arabs. Now I am on the other side. I am more comfortable with the youth group of "Betar*" and my political ideas are more clear.

I thought things could work out, but I was wrong. You know that before I did not hate the Arabs because I didn't think you were capable of such terrible acts. One day, in my neighborhood, an Arab killed people that I knew: a policeman, the florist, and a female soldier who was eighteen years old. Even though they weren't in my family, it hurt me badly. That night when I came home on the little streets, I was terrified. Even now I'm afraid when I go that way. But who isn't afraid on the streets of Jerusalem at night after all? Nevertheless, I have no intention of leaving my country. On the contrary, I would never be able to leave Jerusalem. This is our land, after all. A long time ago it was the Arabs who invaded us first. I think we all should be prepared to defend our country at all times.

I do not agree with the girls who don't serve in the army. I will certainly do my military service when I finish school. Besides, without the army I wouldn't even have been born since that is where my parents met.

Now, like you, I know about war and I realize that it is neither fair or pleasant to live the way you live. On the one hand I understand, but on the other hand, I tell myself that it is your people who are responsible. Each time there is a curfew, that means there has been a murder. It makes sense that you are controlled to avoid disturbances and gatherings.

We don't meet Arabs anymore other than our gardener and sometimes the vegetable seller in Baka. But I trust them because everyone has known them for a long time, and if they were dangerous, people would know it.

You may understand, but you are still an Arab. Because of this, I don't think we can be friends one day.

Galit

March 19, 1991

—◄○►—

The Israeli prime minister objects to the American proposals that require Israel to withdraw from the occupied territories in exchange for peace, because, he claims, the territories in question are part of Eretz Yisrael, the land of Israel.

Israeli Ami Popper, twenty-two years old, is sentenced to seven life sentences in prison for killing seven Palestinians and trying to massacre more. On May 20, 1990, he took the submachine gun from his brother, a soldier on leave, and opened fire on a group of Palestinian workers without any motivation other than blind hate. Popper had no political connections and pleaded insanity, but the court psychiatrists found him competent to stand trial.

Dheisheh
19 March 1991

Dear Galit,
    I have to tell you what upset me in your letter. You said you couldn't be friends anymore with a Palestinian girl. Your decision seems to be hasty. Your ideas hurt me. I'll explain it to you. You judge the Palestinians without knowing what they think, without discussing with them the reasons why they pushed to take part in the Gulf War. We defended Saddam because he supports the Palestinian cause and has promised us our independence.

You say that the Arabs took your land and that you can't live anywhere else than Jerusalem. But the day will come when the Jews will have to live elsewhere and leave Jerusalem and Palestine. You say you want to live in Jerusalem. I can't see myself anywhere but in Palestine. You said you lived for days in fear because of Saddam's missiles; we have lived like that for years. And the more time that it takes, the more determined the Palestinians become.

I don't think your decision will help to achieve peace, but if we spent some time together we would exchange our ideas; we could discuss lots of things.

I really want to see you and speak with you. Tell me if you agree.

In Dheisheh, during the war, we spent the whole time under a curfew. We didn't have the right to go out and do our shopping. We weren't sure we would have enough food. In our house we did not have a sealed room like you did. It is true that when Saddam shot the missiles we went out to look at them and I was happy. I hoped he would win the war to liberate Palestine from the Jews. He wanted to teach a lesson to the other countries in the Gulf that they should stop asking for aid from the West.

Right after the war, we moved out and went to live on the hillside across from us. Dheisheh is finished for us. My father sold the house because my grandfather offered us the ground floor of his house. We haven't finished fixing it up; we still have the garden and the terrace to complete. The whole family works on it without any food all day because it is Ramadan. Life is so different from Dheisheh!

I feel freer here. It's like the country. From the terrace I can see the whole Dheisheh camp. The soldiers standing guard on the roofs of the houses seem tiny. We also have a very pretty view of Bethlehem.

The military outpost is right below us, but the army doesn't come near us very much. We can't do too much here. There are no demonstrations. But I still won't forget the Palestinian cause. I am waiting to be older to demonstrate in the streets.

I will be an outlaw and I won't be afraid when the soldiers hit us and shoot at us. Besides, I have already been hit by a rubber bullet in the knee. It hurt a lot all night, but I was proud to suffer for our freedom. Luckily I was wearing pants and I don't have a scar.

Don't you find adolescence to be a hard age? I don't feel grown up, but I don't feel little. In the house my mother asks me to do more than before. Aside from washing the dishes and straightening the house, I have also learned how to make the bread.

I still go to the school in the camp and I see my old friends. We used to go together to the Movement of Palestinian Women of Dheisheh. We sang and we acted theater pieces. Now that our house is far and I have less free time, I almost never go to the meetings. I learn Palestinian songs from the radio or I listen to my father's cassettes.

Not long ago, my uncle got out of prison. Now it

is my uncle Jawdat who is having problems. They
closed his press bureau again. We don't know why
or for how long. He's the one who told me he'd
take me to Jerusalem one day; there's no way I could
go alone.

Of course, the curfew has to be lifted for us to
get through the military roadblock.

The day when we see each other for the first time,
I wonder if we will be able to speak to each other.
But at least we can look at each other. I can see myself
in your house and imagine you in mine. To meet
will surely be difficult for the two of us, or very simple
if we really want peace.

Write me. I am anxious to see you.

Mervet

P.S. If you answer, tell me how things are going at
your house.

March 31, 1991

◄○►

The first American anti-Scud missiles, known as Patriot missiles, sent over during the war to support the Israeli defenses against the Iraqis, have left the country. In Toulkarem, in the occupied territories, a seventeen-year-old Palestinian, Iyad Ibrahim, was killed when he tried to attack an Israeli soldier with a hatchet. The soldier was slightly wounded.

The death, four days ago, of an Israeli settler killed by a bullet in an ambush is raised in the government council. After a sharp debate, the government adopts a new series of severe measures to combat the Palestinian revolt: Palestinian workers are forbidden to travel in private cars, and militants suspected of terrorist activity will either be expelled or have their homes destroyed.

The conditions of life in the territories are more difficult.

A superhuman effort seems to be necessary to bring the different protagonists to the negotiation table.

Jerusalem
31 March 1991

Dear Mervet,

You asked me for news about my family. It is sad news. My father died after a long illness; he had lung cancer.

But I have a few more cheerful memories of this

time. Tally got married and I will be an aunt in September! She got married in the Moroccan wedding dress that my mother and grandmother wore and that I hope I will wear someday. Last fall I had my Bat Mitzvah. We had a party at the moshav with the whole family. I have a videocassette of the party that I watch from time to time.

For the last few months, I feel more adult. At home I am more and more responsible for Irit and Yael. I often go walking in town. I have decided to become a designer. I use a little makeup, just lipstick.

I read your letter and I was pretty disappointed. Like you were hoping for me, I was hoping for more from you.

I thought a lot about it. I know that you were chased off your land and that you are unhappy, but if you behaved differently, our relationship would be better. If the Arabs didn't throw stones, we would not shoot at them. Obviously, violence promotes violence, especially when you take revenge on innocent people.

I'm okay about meeting you on condition that you come to Jerusalem. I have kept your picture and could recognize you in the street even though after all this time you have certainly changed.

Next Saturday, if you want, I will wait for you at the home of my uncle, who lives in an area where no one can see us. My uncle is called Zvi, but in the family we call him Shlomo, his name from Morocco.

His house is just above an Arab village, and he gets along well with them.

Today I am skeptical, but I continue to hope that one day there will be peace in the country. I am ready to compromise, to talk to the Arabs, even with those who kill. When you make compromises you have to do it with everyone. Till Saturday!

Galit

The Meeting

◄O►

April 6, 1991. The Saturday of the "compromise" dawns with heavy rain. Galit feels pulled in different directions because of her decision to meet her Palestinian friend/enemy. That no one will see them in her uncle's out-of-the-way neighborhood calms her a little.

Mervet, on her side, is torn between excitement and apprehension. She sits next to her uncle in the backseat of the taxi that takes them to Jerusalem.

Silently she gazes out the window at the countryside that passes by under the pouring rain.

The taxi passes a checkpoint and is headed toward the holy city.

On the hillside of the Talpiot neighborhood, the Judean sky opens to view. Intimidated, Mervet gets out of the car, and Galit slowly approaches her. She is very elegant looking, dressed all in black. Mervet is dressed in her pretty white jacket, which she saves for special occasions. Smiling, they wave to each other and then squeeze hands. They get past the first moments together. Mervet wipes her eyes; Galit fiddles uncomfortably with her umbrella.

"How old are you now?" Mervet asks in English.

"I'm fourteen years old. And you?" says Galit.

"Fifteen," Mervet responds, staring out at the horizon of the valley, where a rainbow has just appeared. "It's beautiful here."

A few yards away another meeting takes place—that

of the two uncles, Jawdat and Shlomo, a militant Israeli pacifist. The friendly conversation gets to politics right away: the upcoming peace negotiations and U.S. Secretary of State James Baker's recent visit to Jerusalem.

We head to Shlomo's house, situated at the edge of Jerusalem and bordering a Palestinian village. On the way, Jawdat speaks to Galit, and Shlomo astonishes Mervet by speaking to her in Arabic. She understands when he explains that he spent his childhood in Morocco, and she searches her memory for the word *Sephardic,* which includes both their roots. Galit makes tea and is surprised when Mervet politely refuses the little cakes; it is the middle of Ramadan!

Tea is therefore served after sunset in a beautiful silver teapot from Morocco. It is the moment to exchange gifts. Galit receives a Palestinian bracelet braided by Mervet. The young Israeli puts it on right away but is careful to hide it under the sleeve of her jacket. The compromises continue. For her turn, she gives Mervet a drawing of the flags of their two nations. The Palestinian flag is not yet finished. Galit had outlined the shapes, but she admits that she does not know the colors. Mervet colors her drawing before taking it home.

Each one has come with her camera, a gift I gave both of them last year. The souvenir photo of each one is taken with a flash. Night fell long ago.

Months later, toward the end of October 1991, the first Middle East peace negotiations take place in Madrid. I feel Galit and Mervet are involved, and yet the negotiations are far removed from them.

Today, I don't know if Galit has changed her anti-Palestinian opinions. Nor do I know what vengeance Mervet is planning against Israel. Hundreds of miles away, the peace discussions between the Israelis and the Palestinians continue. So does the war.

TWO PEOPLES AND ONE LAND:
A Historical Overview

The Israeli-Palestinian relationship is a history of love and hate. Love for the same land and hate for the "other" people. On one side are the Jews, on the other, the Arabs.

Today, the first have a country, the latter assert their claim for theirs. The tragedy comes from the fact that each considers the country to be theirs, and theirs alone. In Hebrew it is called Eretz Yisrael—the land of Israel; in Arabic, Filastine—Palestine.

Two Thousand Years Ago . . .

The Jews lost their independence and their country two thousand years ago in a hopeless war against the Romans. By the tens of thousands, the survivors sought refuge in bordering countries. Others were taken as prisoners of war and sold in Rome at the slave market. Since that ancient time, the descendants of these first exiles scattered across the continents, sometimes tolerated, sometimes chased out. This exodus is called the "Diaspora."

During this time, the Jews' former land was passed from hand to hand, always coveted and conquered by military force, changing its name according to the conquerors.

Leaving Jerusalem, the exiled Jews promised to return, repeating from the Bible: "If I forget thee, O Jerusalem, let my right hand forget her cunning." And each one added: "Next year in Jerusalem."

Although the prayer for return was, for a long time, a

religious expression, Jews the world over have kept the memory of this destiny.

Until the middle of the nineteenth century, the number of Jews who made the return trip was very small, but it was enough to maintain a Jewish presence in the land of Israel.

1897: The First International Jewish Congress

The rise of anti-Semitism, as well as the increase of pogroms* in eastern Europe, made conditions favorable for the appearance of a nonreligious movement in the hearts of European Jews. This movement's main goal was the return of the Jewish people to Israel, their country of origin, also known as Zion. This is the origin for the name of the movement: Zionism.

The Dreyfus Affair, which exploded in France in 1894, was, without doubt, one of the determining factors in the Jewish recognition of the necessity for a Zionist movement.

A young Jewish French army captain, Alfred Dreyfus, on the general staff of the army, was wrongly accused of being a traitor. His trial caused a judicial and political scandal, pitting the anti-Dreyfusards, right-wing, anti-Semitic nationalists, against the Dreyfusards, left-wing, nonreligious republicans. Condemned for spying by the war council, Dreyfus was exiled to Guiana. Three years later it became clear that the real villain was another officer on the general staff, Count Esterhazy.

Esterhazy was not found guilty, however. At the retrial, Dreyfus was again found guilty, then finally pardoned in 1899. The scandal continued until 1906, the year he was cleared of all charges.

The Dreyfus Affair had a big impact on Zionism, through the intermediary of a young Jewish Hungarian journalist,

Theodor Herzl. A Paris correspondent for a Viennese newspaper, *Neue Freie Press,* he reported every day on the latest developments of the Dreyfus Affair. "Our place, a place for all Jews," wrote the young journalist, "must be respected and defended. But this will not be possible unless we have our own land, a Country like everyone else. A Country which would be defended by international law and recognized by the other countries." Herzl developed his program in a pamphlet titled *The Jewish State.*

In 1897, in the Swiss city of Basel, he convoked the first Zionist Congress, uniting all those who, in the heart of the Jewish communities of Europe and America, aspired to the creation of a national homeland in Palestine. In his journal, Herzl declared, "In Basel, I founded the Jewish state."

A half century later, his dream was realized and Herzl was declared the "Father of the Jewish State," but he would never know it: he died in 1904 at age forty-four, following a serious illness.

For centuries the Jews fled persecution by migrating from one European country to another. In 1881 new pogroms in Russia pushed the Jews to leave the "old country": more than two million sought refuge in America, while for the first time in two thousand years, a very modest parallel movement was drawn to Palestine.

In the 1930s massacres in Ukraine pushed almost two hundred thousand Jews to move to Palestine. During World War II and as a result of the Holocaust, three hundred thousand Jewish refugees took the same path.

Today still, after the fall of the Communist regime, the fear of rising anti-Semitism seems to encourage many Russian Jews to immigrate to Israel.

1917: The British Conquest of Palestine and the Balfour Declaration

At the beginning of the twentieth century, of all the major powers, only Britain looked favorably on the settlement of Jews in Palestine.

In 1917 the British army entered Palestine, chasing the Ottoman army from Jerusalem; several Jewish battalions fought under the British flag.

In London, in the course of a diplomatic ceremony, the secretary of the foreign office, Lord Balfour, expressed his "sympathy for the goals of the Zionists Jews." On November 2, 1917, he affirmed he would "favorably consider the establishment of a homeland for the Jewish people in Palestine." His Majesty's government began to promote the realization of this project. The Balfour Declaration was approved by the League of Nations, which was created in 1919 and replaced by the United Nations in 1945. In 1922 the League of Nations gave Great Britain the responsibility for the administration of Palestine.

The winds of hope blew across the Middle East. The fall of the Ottoman Empire brought about the realization of the dreams of the Arab peoples, who had lived in the region for centuries, to free themselves from the Ottoman yoke and create an independent state, redefining Syria, Lebanon, and Palestine.

In the beginning, the Arabs were hospitable to the Jews. The Arabs were ruled by the Hashemites, a desert dynasty from Arabia, who had become, with the help of the British, very influential in the Arab world at the beginning of the nineteenth century. In 1917, King Hussein of Hejaz went so far as to invite the Jews to return to their "beloved holy land." His son, Emir Faysal, met the head of the Zionists,

Chaim Weitzmann, in Aqaba. "We are struggling for Arab independence," the emir declared to Weitzmann, "and we would be unbrotherly if we did not say to the Jews—as I am doing—welcome."

But it would not be so simple. France and Great Britain disagreed about the division of the ancient Ottoman lands. In the end, Emir Faysal was not, as he had hoped and as the British had promised him, monarch of a great Syrian kingdom, within which the Jews would find their place.

In Palestine, Arab nationalism became militant, not only struggling against British colonialism but also against the Jews recently arrived from Europe. The socialist ideas of these westerners upset the traditional Arab society and only heightened the conflict between the two communities.

The first "nationalist" clashes soon exploded. In May 1921 riots bloodied the Tel Aviv region, resulting in about one hundred victims, nearly all Jews. Fighting continued over the years. The British investigative commission appointed to examine these events fed the rupture between the mandate's authorities and the Yishuv, the Jewish community in Palestine. The rupture was complete after the publication of the first MacDonald White Paper in 1939, a government report prescribing extreme measures against the Jews in Palestine. Most notably, the British severely limited any new Jewish immigration. Realizing the degree of Arab discontent, the British sought to limit the effects of the Balfour Declaration. This change of attitude damaged the relationships between the Zionists and the British, as well as the Zionists and the Palestinians.

1929: The Husseini, or the Nationalists, Are the Victors

In the Palestinian camp, two big families, the Nashashibi and the Husseini, fought over power. The Nashashibi, westernized and moderate, had relatively good relations with the British and the Jews.

In the early 1920s, they represented a considerable political force. Raghib Bey, head of the Nashashibi and leader of the National Party, was the mayor of Jerusalem and presided over an era of building and modernization in the city.

The Husseini were nationalistic traditional Muslims. The most famous was Hadj Amin al-Husseini, the grand mufti of Jerusalem, charged with maintaining religious law. He was the chief of the Arab High Committee, a quasi-official Arab government, the most savage enemy of the Jewish colonization. More than once, his appeals provoked violent anti-Jewish riots. For Hadj Amin al-Husseini, there was no room in this Muslim land for either the English or the Jews.

Saturday, August 24, 1929, at Hadj Amin's urging, Arab rioters attacked the Jews in Hebron and massacred sixty-seven men, women, and children, and wounded more than a hundred; the synagogues were plundered. The survivors fled the city, putting an end to the two-thousand-year Jewish presence in the city. The British appointed a new investigative committee. Among the recommendations: limit Jewish immigration and land purchases.

In the Palestinian camp, the Husseini won a definitive victory over the Nashashibi and opened hostilities against Great Britain and the Zionists. In 1936 the "Arab Revolt" exploded and lasted three years. The British army sent reinforcements against the Arab revolutionaries. The Haganah*, the Jewish military organization, created a secret army.

(87)

1937: The Peel Commission

In 1937 the British sent a new royal commission to the region: the Peel Commission. As a result of its report, the authorities decided to disband the Arab High Committee, arrest its leaders, and exile them to the Seychelles in the Indian Ocean.

Hadj Amin al-Husseini escaped arrest and took refuge first in Syria and then in Iraq. His hatred of Jews brought him to Berlin, where, in 1941, he offered to collaborate with Hitler.

But the Peel Commission made another recommendation, which aimed to satisfy the Jews and Arabs and would resolve, once and for all, the conflict between the two peoples. It proposed to divide Palestine into a Jewish state and a Palestinian state and to maintain a British enclave around Jerusalem. The Jewish leaders accepted the plan; the Arabs rejected it. The idea of dividing the territory would be raised again ten years later.

At the end of World War II, the horrors revealed by the discovery of concentration camps in Poland and Germany, in which six million Jewish men, women, and children, along with millions of other victims of German fascism, perished, made it imperative that a Jewish state be created in Palestine. On the other hand, in 1945, the Arab League, which had just been organized, affirmed its determination to maintain an Arab Palestine.

In 1946 the British refused to let the Jewish survivors of the Holocaust enter Palestine. This provoked a wave of anti-British Zionist terrorism in Palestine and international public incomprehension. As a result, Great Britain decided to put the Palestine question before the United Nations.

1948: The Birth of the State of Israel

On November 29, 1947, by a majority of thirty-three countries to thirteen, with ten abstentions, the general assembly of the United Nations recommended dividing Palestine between the Jews and the Arabs. This was Resolution 181. Hearing the results of the vote, the six hundred thousand Jews of Palestine danced in the streets.

The council of the Arab League threatened to oppose the plan with force. Groups of militant Arabs from neighboring countries infiltrated the country to intensify the guerrilla tactics against the Jews. A virtual war was engaged before the independent state of Israel could even be declared.

On May 14, 1948, the day the British Mandate withdrew from Palestine, the creation of the State of Israel was proclaimed in Tel Aviv and was soon recognized by the United Nations. A provisionary government was named under the leadership of David Ben-Gurion. But Israel was immediately invaded by the regular troops of Egypt, Syria, Jordan, and Lebanon, in addition to contingents from Saudi Arabia and Sudan. The Egyptian armed divisions were less than twenty miles south of Tel Aviv, the Israeli capital. The Iraqi forces, arriving from the east, threatened to cut Israel in half at the height of Tel Aviv, and to isolate the northern half of the country. They were only nine miles from the sea to the west. The Jordanian troops encircled Jerusalem, and in the north, Syrians and Lebanese advanced rapidly on the hills of Galilee.

Faced with armed divisions, artillery, and the Arab air forces, Israel hastily drafted thirty thousand civilians. They had neither artillery nor tanks or military airplanes. But they fought with the spirit of despair, convinced they had to beat the Arabs or all be killed. The crushing superiority of the Arab forces turned out to be more theoretical than actual.

The Israelis took the offensive, equipped with modern weapons bought from abroad.

After two years of fighting, the war ended. The price of independence was heavy: sixty-five hundred Jews killed, or almost one out of every hundred Israelis. The numbers were higher for the Arabs.

In 1949 a cease-fire accord was reached between Israel and Egypt, Syria, and Jordan. The Israeli territory was now one-third larger than the United Nations' version. For the first time since the beginning of the conflict, the Jews were the majority in their land.

While Israel gained its independence, some 700,000 Palestinians lost their houses and their country. Having left the combat zones for safer Arab territories, they thought they would return at the end of the war. Their leaders and the heads of Arab states had promised that the war would not be long and that, at its conclusion, Zionism would only be a bad memory and they would return home.

But the war ended differently. Several of the evacuated regions were now inside the Israeli borders. Of the 750,000 Arabs who, before the war, lived in land now owned by the State of Israel, only 150,000 remained and became Israeli citizens. The others, about 600,000, were crowded into refugee camps.

Palestinian society is semifeudal and agricultural; the chiefs, members of the important families, owned most of the cultivated land and held the political power. Their wealth and their contacts in the neighboring countries allowed them to settle relatively easily in exile.

The poor people did less well. The refugee camps were established in anguish and misery.

At the same time, the State of Israel, which gathered in nearly six hundred thousand Jews from Arab countries, accused its neighbors of deliberately maintaining the disastrous condition of the Palestinian refugees by blocking the humanitarian efforts of the United Nations. Ralph Galloway, the former director of UNRWA, condemned this policy: "The Arab countries do not wish to resolve the problem of the refugees. They want them to remain like an open wound, an affront to the United Nations and a weapon against Israel. Whether these refugees live or die, the Arab leaders couldn't care less."

But this was not the essential. The refugees never gave up their claim to their national identity and their homeland.

Only Jordan, which annexed the West Bank—a portion of the territory east of the Jordan River, designated part of the Arab territory in the United Nations plan—gave citizenship to the Palestinians and integrated them into its economy. A large portion of these Palestinians would come under the Israeli occupation in 1967, when Jordan lost this territory in the Six-Day War.

The long tragedy of the refugees became, after the question of territory, the most burning and most difficult issue to resolve in the Arab-Israeli conflict.

1950: Gearing Up for Violence

In the beginning of the 1950s, the fedayeen—Palestinian fighters—infiltrated Israel through the West Bank. Their incursions, which became more and more frequent and deadly, sowed terror in the Israeli border villages. In 1951, 137 Israelis of all ages were killed by the fedayeen. In 1952 there were 147 deaths, and the following year, 180; most were civilians.

The Israeli response was always spectacular and brutal. A

special commando group of parachutists, Unit 101, was formed to operate beyond the borders. The leader, Ariel Sharon, a young officer who would one day be a general and then defense minister, individually selected the forty men in the commando group.

On October 13, 1953, a grenade thrown by the fedayeen into the interior of a house near the border in Tirat-Yehuda killed a Jewish woman and her two children. Four other children were wounded. The suspects were thought to be from Kibya, a Palestinian village on the other side of the border. That night, Unit 101 silently entered the village and blew up forty-five houses with dynamite. Sixty-six men, women, and children were killed and seventy-five were wounded. The operation was sharply criticized by Israeli public opinion. The government claimed that the reprisal was financed by the Tirat-Yehuda villagers. Unit 101 was nevertheless dismantled.

In March 1954 a group of fedayeen machine-gunned an Israeli bus on the road to Eilat. The outcome: eleven killed and twenty wounded. There was a spiral of violence: after the massacre, the Israeli army retaliated with an attack against a police post on the other side of the border.

In the Gaza Strip, then under Egyptian control, the Palestinian fedayeen who lived in the refugee camps were, for the most part, armed and trained by the Egyptian army. Their increasingly frequent incursions made daily life impossible for the Israelis who lived in the southern part of the country. In retaliation, the Israeli army launched a series of nocturnal attacks against the Palestinian camps and the Egyptian army outposts.

October 1956: War Between Israel and Egypt

Opposed to the nationalization of the Suez Canal by Egyptian President Gamal Abdel Nasser, France and Great Britain decided to join forces with Israel and sent troops to the banks of the canal. Israel occupied the Gaza Strip and the immense Sinai Desert, but withdrew several months later under pressure from the United States, which was trying to calm tensions in the Middle East.

1967: The Six-Day War

War broke out again in June 1967. In response to new threats from Nasser, the Israeli army launched a lightning attack on the Suez Canal, then confronted the Jordanian army and took the Golan Heights from Syria, a strategic position from which the Syrian army shot at Israeli villages from the hills. In the first hours of the day, the Israeli air force destroyed nearly all the Egyptian air force, which was still on the ground, permitting the army to turn back the Syrian, Jordanian, and Egyptian forces. The conquered territory was four times the size of the State of Israel: the Gaza Strip, the Sinai Desert, East Jerusalem, the West Bank, and the Golan Heights.

As a result, the United Nations adopted Resolution 242. This required that Israel return all of the occupied territories in exchange for recognition by the Arab countries of the Jewish state. Today, the resolution is still unfulfilled.

While 250,000 Palestinians fled the west bank of the Jordan river, about one million more, as well as several thousand Druzes, several thousand Bedouins, and Syrian and Egyptian citizens came under Israeli occupation.

The Armed Struggle Intensifies

In 1964 the creation of the Palestine Liberation Organization (PLO), which brought together the various Palestinian organizations, gave a structure to the fedayeen and intensified the armed struggle against the Jewish state. While the Israelis declared themselves ready to negotiate a compromise with the Arab states, they refused to recognize the existence of a Palestinian people. For the leaders of the Jewish state, the Palestinians were Arabs who had to integrate themselves into the neighboring Arab countries, and the PLO was a terrorist organization that had to be eliminated.

The PLO showed itself to be as inflexible as Israel. It claimed the liberation of the entire territory of Palestine and called for the destruction of the State of Israel.

In the euphoria of victory, the Israelis spoke of a "humanitarian occupation" of the territories, as if such a concept, contradictory in its very description, was possible. "We will live in security," they said, "and the Arabs will benefit from an increase in their standard of living, while we will profit from labor that we lack."

In the refugee camps, the Fatah cells, the principal organizers of the PLO, mobilized against the Israeli military and Israeli civilians, and also against any Palestinians who collaborated with the occupation. The Palestinian attacks and the Israeli retaliations continued in waves for twenty years.

Car bombs; explosives set off in markets, movie theaters, and bus stops; the shelling of border villages; hostage taking; and mail bombs created many victims.

The terrorism became international: Japanese terrorists, in the name of the Palestinians, assassinated Israeli and foreign travelers at Tel Aviv's airport. Palestinian groups also attacked the airplanes of El Al, the Israeli airline, hijacking a plane to Algiers and blowing up a plane in midair. Then, when security for El Al flights became too efficient, they turned to European and American airline companies in hopes of alerting the entire world to the situation of the Palestinian people.

Eventually the bloody conflicts became an open war, the Yom Kippur War of 1973. In this war, the Arabs launched a major attack on Yom Kippur, the most holy day of the Israeli year. Despite being taken by surprise when most Israelis were in synagogue praying, the Israelis rallied and defeated the Arabs.

Is Armed Conflict the Only Solution?

The question was posed publicly in Arabic in the occupied territories and also in Hebrew. At the margins of the terrorist activities, a genuine revolution was taking place in the heart of Palestinian society. The traditional leaders and the notables had disappeared, leaving an ideological void at a national level. It was filled by the young university-educated Palestinians who became the new generation of leaders. These intellectuals did not come from the ranks of the bourgeoisie, the middle class, but from more modest backgrounds, including the refugee camps. For the first time, a new Palestinian elite had emerged, desirous of taking charge of its national destiny.

1977: A First Step Toward Peace

The Egyptian president, Anwar el-Sadat, successor to Nasser, came to Jerusalem to meet the Israeli prime minister, Menachem Begin, and gave a speech at the Knesset, the Israeli parliament. This event led to the Camp David peace accord of 1979, the first peace treaty between an Arab country and Israel. Egypt regained the territory conquered by Israel in 1967. This accord was denounced by the other Arab states and the PLO. If this agreement, signed under the protection of the United States, sealed peace between the Egyptians and Israelis, it settled nothing for the Palestinians.

But before the Israelis and Palestinians could take the smallest steps toward peace, another form of war broke out. It did not resemble the preceding wars, in which regular, well-equipped armies clashed. This new battle was named the "War of the Stones," the intifada.

1987: The Intifada

It exploded on December 9, 1987, in the Palestinian village of Gaza, where three days earlier, an Israeli merchant had been stabbed. The day after the murder, an Israeli truck collided with a private car, killing the driver and three of his passengers, from the Palestinian camp of Jabalya. The residents of the camp were convinced that the accident was a premeditated act. At the funerals, residents burned tires and attacked an Israeli army patrol. The soldiers shot into the crowd. One Palestinian was killed and sixteen were wounded.

At night calm returned to the narrow streets of Jabalya. The army thought that the day's riot would only be another bad memory among many others.

But this time the incidents started again the next day and spread like wildfire in the Gaza Strip and then to the West Bank. The residents attacked the Israeli military with stones, iron bars, and Molotov cocktails. The Israeli army reacted strongly. Not a day passed without wounded and dead among the Palestinians.

The Israeli army classified the situation as very serious and sent reinforcements with orders to calm the chaos. But the Palestinians refused to return to the old status quo.

On January 1, the anniversary of the creation of Fatah, the Palestinians decided to increase the level of violence against the military. A secret order decreed a general strike in all the occupied territories. The riots took on a new dimension. In several locations, hundreds of thousands of demonstrators opposed the army from dawn on. Children from seven to fifteen years old were on the front lines. They collected stones and threw them at the military. To disperse the rioters, the Israeli soldiers received permission to fire into the air. But some shot into the crowd. The scenes became more frequent and more and more violent. Eight Palestinians died the first week; hundreds were wounded. Israeli spokespersons judged that these were "unimportant disturbances" provoked, as Prime Minister Yitzhak Shamir put it, "by ruffians and criminals who know that the Israeli army makes every effort not to make victims." The Palestinians responded more vigorously. Combat units, usually deployed on the borders, were sent in to help. The soldiers were ordered to open fire "in case of danger." Officers could order arrests and expulsions.

The Shin Bet, the Israeli secret service, received the order to use any methods necessary to quell the riots. Its agents put together lists of Palestinians thought to be troublemakers. In a single night, around two hundred Palestinians were arrested and sent to Ansar, a new detention camp built in the desert. Ten days after Fatah's anniversary, the toll was twenty-two dead Palestinians and more than nine hundred held at Ansar.

The demonstrations and clashes continued over the weeks and months that followed. They were especially violent on Friday, the day of prayer for Muslims. At the call of the muezzin, faithful Muslims kneel and pray five times a day, facing Mecca. On Friday at noon they go to the mosque to participate in prayer before hearing the imam's preaching.

In the occupied territories, from the beginning of the intifada, the imams' lectures had been almost exclusively about the conflict. Often, the crowds exiting from the prayer session erupted in rioting. The intifada was becoming a religious war that ceaselessly built the wall of hatred.

The hatred of some nourishes the hatred of others. Professor Moubarak Awad, like other Palestinian intellectuals, knows this logic well. An immigrant to the United States, he returned to Jerusalem in 1984 to create and direct a research center dedicated to nonviolent resistance. His model was the legendary Mahatma Gandhi, who led India to independence through a campaign of nonviolent civic disobedience against the British.

After the second week of riots, Awad suggested to his brothers nonviolent resistance against the Israeli occupation.

First, he proposed boycotting Israeli products, then contact with authorities. This would not threaten to sink Israeli industry, but it would show that the Palestinians were determined to have their independence. Moubarak Awad, an American citizen with a tourist visa, was deported from Israel on the pretext that his visitor's permit had expired.

His followers continued his work. "An army can conquer another army," they said to the young militants of the intifada, "but an army cannot conquer an entire people who go out in the streets for their independence." The *chababs* and Moubarak Awad had introduced a new form of confrontation in the endless war between the Israelis and the Palestinians.

What is civil disobedience? It is difficult to explain the theory, but easy to give an example. In Beit Sahur, a Palestinian town of eight thousand inhabitants on the hills of the West Bank, they do not throw stones or Molotov cocktails. From the first days of the uprising, the inhabitants, most of whom belong to the Greek Orthodox Church, rarely went into the streets. Maybe because Beit Sahur is one of the wealthiest and best educated of the Palestinian territories, the residents of Beit Sahur brandished financial weapons against the occupation: they refused to pay taxes to the Israeli authorities. In February 1987, ten months before the start of the intifada, the merchants and other taxpayers of Beit Sahur paid 2.2 million shekels—about $1.25 million—to the Israeli tax collectors. A year later, once Professor Awad's ideas on civil disobedience had been adopted and the order was given to break off relations with Israeli authorities, Beit Sahur followed the plan to the letter: the Palestinians who were policemen resigned from the Israeli police force, drivers refused to pay their registrations, and merchants their taxes.

Beit Sahur created a parallel administration. Local doctors and nurses organized a health care service, and teachers taught classes to students whose schools had been closed, while action committees supervised the plan. An agronomist taught the residents how to convert their gardens into vegetable patches.

For the first months the Israeli administration did not react to the boycott. But when Beit Sahur became an example for the other Palestinian settlements, tax collectors made a raid on the town. At dawn on July 8, 1988, accompanied by the military, the tax collectors went from house to house, confiscating electrical appliances, furniture, and work tools. Despite this attempt to intimidate them, the citizens of Beit Sahur still refused to pay taxes. Other villages followed Beit Sahur's example.

For several years the Israelis have tried to end the intifada: they have declared a curfew several times in the entire occupied territories, arresting tens of thousands of Palestinians and expelling dozens of activists. But in vain. The harder the Israelis try to stop the intifada, the more it grows.

The conclusion seems inevitable: the solution is not in the use of force, but in political negotiations.

Despite considerable military strength, the Israeli government is incapable of ending the uprising; on the other hand, the head of the PLO, Yassir Arafat, who for twenty-three years has headed an organization bent on armed struggle, is ready to take a step toward dialogue.

In Algeria, on November 15, 1988, Yassir Arafat read a long proclamation named the Declaration of Independence for the State of Palestine. Recapping the history of the conflict, Arafat referred to the United Nations resolutions establishing the legitimacy of the Palestinian people. This time he did not speak of rights "to" Palestine, but "in" Palestine. At the United Nations, the PLO chief declared recognition of the existence of the State of Israel and renounced terrorism. The PLO proposed a plan to divide Palestine. It also recognized Resolution 242 as the basis of peace negotiations between Israel and the Palestinians.

Most of the territories in question are still under Israeli control, and there is no thought yet of turning them over to the Palestinians. Nevertheless the joy was great. In Algiers, as in the occupied territories, red, black, and green helium balloons were released. These are the colors of the Palestinian flag.

"We can finally put an end to the violence to institute an era of coexistence between our two peoples," declared a leader of the intifada in Jerusalem. But the immediate reaction of the Israeli leaders left no room for illusions. "We

(100)

don't believe a single word of it," retorted Prime Minister Yitzhak Shamir. Suspicion bred of a century of conflict would not be so quickly forgotten.

With the fall of communism in Eastern Europe, the end of the cold war, and the demise of the Soviet Union, Israel's Arab neighbors lost their major ally. The balance of power in the Middle East began to change.

The Gulf War was the proof. August 1990: Iraq invaded Kuwait. A military coalition under the direction of the United States realigned the western countries as well as certain Arab countries, most notably Syria, Egypt, and Saudi Arabia.

Although the UN's goal for this coalition was to liberate Kuwait, the Palestinian question very soon came to the fore.

Soon after the Gulf War, the United States, the only influential power in the Middle East, pushed to assemble the Arab countries, the Israelis, and the Palestinians at the peace table to negotiate.

On October 30, 1991, in Madrid, Spain, delegates from Israel, Palestine, Syria, Lebanon, and Jordan instituted direct negotiations that would put an end to the bloody Middle East conflict that had existed for so long.

Jews and Arabs both knew that these negotiations would take a long time.

But never had there been such a good chance for peace. The majority of the countries affirmed their determination to guide the peace negotiations between Israel and its neighbors, to create the best chance to achieve peace.

GLOSSARY

administrative detention: a punitive measure inherited from the British protectorate. When Israel decrees a state of emergency in the occupied territories, security personnel can arrest anyone for an unspecified amount of time without normal judicial process. A general's signature is all that is needed. No proof of guilt is provided. The detained can appeal to the civil court, but only the judge has access to the charges. Since the intifada, the maximum period of detention has doubled from six to twelve months. About four thousand Palestinians have been subjected to this measure.

Allahou akbar ("God is great"): a Muslim religious expression that is often repeated in prayers and also in daily conversation. It is with these words that the muezzin begins his call to prayer. Since the intifada, "Allahou akbar" has also become a war cry of the Palestinian revolt.

army: at eighteen all Israelis, male and female, are required to perform military service. Very religious Jews have a religious exemption and do not serve.

Ashdod: a medium-size port city south of Tel Aviv. Its working-class neighborhoods and housing developments contribute to its poor reputation.

Ashkenazi: Jews from Eastern Europe, especially from Germany, Poland, Austria, and Russia.

Bar/Bat Mitzvah: Jewish ceremony that is usually celebrated at thirteen years for boys (Bar Mitzvah) and, in Israel, at twelve for girls (Bat Mitzvah). The ceremony marks the time when a child is considered an adult and can participate in religious rituals. The family often has a party for friends and family.

Betar: an Israeli youth movement of the nationalist right wing, which supports the annexation of the occupied territories.

Birzeit University: the Palestinian university north of Jerusalem. The students and some of the professors are known for being militant supporters of a Palestinian state and are active in the intifada.

bus 405: this bus follows a route that connects the two largest cities in Israel—Tel Aviv and Jerusalem. On July 7, 1989, a Palestinian passenger armed with a knife seized the steering wheel and drove the bus into the bottom of a ravine. Sixteen Israeli passengers were killed and twenty-five more were wounded.

chababs: young Palestinian militants of the intifada. They are between twelve and twenty-five years old.

chahid ("martyr" in Arabic): all Palestinians who have died for the intifada are declared chahid. They are said to be assured eternal life in paradise.

circumcise, circumcision: a religious rite that symbolizes the alliance with God. It consists of removing the foreskin of a boy's penis. It is performed on Muslims before they are thirteen years old and on Jewish infants when they are eight days old.

concentration camps: also known as "death camps." During World War II (1939–1945), the Nazis sought to exterminate the Jews. Concentration camps were mainly built in Poland, where there was the greatest concentration of Jews. Trains brought victims from all over Europe. The most infamous camps were Auschwitz and Treblinka.

Dead Sea: a lake so salty that no fish or microorganism can survive. It is the lowest spot in the world, 1,148 feet below sea level.

(104)

Dheisheh: a refuge camp located on a hillside near the city of Bethlehem and near Jerusalem. About seven thousand Palestinians live in the camp.

Eilat: an important port city situated on the Gulf of Aqaba. It is also a popular tourist destination.

Falashas: Jews from Ethiopia. According to the Bible, they are the descendants of King Solomon and the queen of Sheba. For 2,500 years the Falashas have lived apart from the rest of the Jewish population. Recently, tens of thousands of Falashas have been transferred by airlift from Ethiopia to Israel. Israel saved these severely persecuted African Jews in a series of dramatic rescues.

Fatah: the principal military and political group in the Palestinian Liberation Organization (PLO), considered terrorists in the eyes of the Israelis. The PLO is headed by Yassir Arafat.

Feast of the Sacrifice ("Id el-Adha"): according to Muslim traditions, the patriarch Ibrahim, father of both the Jewish and Arab nations, was about to sacrifice his eldest son, Ishmael, to God. At the moment when Ibrahim was to cut his son's throat, an angel saved the child, and Ibrahim sacrificed a lamb in his son's place. Each year Muslims celebrate this festival by killing a lamb. In the Jewish tradition, as written in the Bible, the patriarch Abraham was about to sacrifice his only legitimate son, Isaac, when the angel intervened to save the child.

Galilee: a mountainous region situated north of Israel. It is less populated than the center of the country. It is the only region where Jews are not in the majority.

general strike: several times, following important events, the Palestinians declared a general strike, paralyzing all activity.

Haganah: a paramilitary organization of Jews in Palestine. The units fought alongside the British during World

War II and made up the core of the new army of the State of Israel in 1948.

Hashomer Hatzair: the youth movement of the militant Israeli left wing that supports the coexistence of Jews and Arabs and supports withdrawal from the occupied territories.

Hasidim: ultraorthodox Jews who dress the same as their ancestors did in Poland. For example, the men wear broad-brimmed hats and long black coats.

Hebron: a Palestinian village and the capital of the region of the same name, south of Jerusalem. Hebron is a sacred area for the Jews. Under the big mosque in the center of town is the Tomb of the Patriarchs, Abraham, Isaac, and Jacob, venerated by Jews and Muslims. The coexistence between the two communities has always been strained, especially since Jewish settlers have chosen to settle near the Tomb of the Patriarchs, in the heart of the Muslim community.

Holocaust: the extermination of Europe's Jews by Hitler's Nazis during World War II (1939–1945). About six million Jews were massacred during the Holocaust.

Ibrahim: the patriarch, Ibrahim (Abraham in the Bible), had several wives. Sarah, his legal wife, was unable to have children. Her servant, Hagar, gave him a son, Ishmael. At the age of one hundred, Sarah welcomed three nomads who promised her that she would have a son. A year later she gave birth to a son named Isaac. Sarah insisted that Abraham send Hagar and Ishmael away into the desert. God reassured Abraham that Ishmael would survive and would become the father of the Arabs.

Id and Fitr: the holiday that marks the end of Ramadan. The Friday before the holiday, Muslims celebrate *Leilat-el-Kadr,* "the night of destiny." That night, the prophet

Mohammed dreamed that he flew on his horse, El-Bourak, from the square at the mosque of Al-Aksa to Jerusalem.

intifada ("the uprising" in Arabic):   a revolt that exploded in December 1987. The intifada is the popular Palestine revolution that, in different forms—strikes, demonstrations, and terrorist attacks—struggles against the Israeli occupation. See the history section for more details.

kaffiyeh: Palestinian traditional head scarf. The young Palestinians of the intifada often use them as a mask to hide their features during confrontations with Israeli soldiers.

Kotel ("the wall" in Hebrew):   the most sacred place for Jews. The wall of lamentations is the last remaining piece of the Second Temple, destroyed by the Romans in A.D. 70.

Kuwait: an oil-rich Arab country situated in the Persian Gulf. Four hundred thousand Palestinians settled in Kuwait to find work. Their wages supported their families in the occupied territories. After the Gulf War in 1991, Kuwait forcibly returned the Palestinians to Jordan.

milouim: the military reserve service that each Israeli must complete once a year, every year, until age fifty-four. Since the beginning of the intifada, the length of *milouim* has been extended and varies between three and six months. Regular army service begins at eighteen years. It lasts two years for girls and three years for boys.

Molotov cocktail: a bottle or container filled with flammable explosives and fitted with a wick, usually a rag, that is lit. When thrown, it breaks and sets fire where it lands.

moshav: Israeli agricultural village based on a cooperative social system. Each family works its own farm, but the purchase of machines and the distribution of the crops is done communally.

muezzin: a religious man charged with calling the Muslim faithful to the five daily prayer sessions of Islam. The muezzin calls from the top of the minaret on the mosque.

Negev: a desert area in the south of Israel.

new immigrants (*olim hadashim* in Hebrew): the State of Israel has a law found in no other country. It recognizes that all Jews are entitled to Israeli citizenship and have the right to settle in Israel. The new arrivals are called "new immigrants." When a Jew emigrates to Israel, it is called making *aliyah*, "to rise up." When they settle, the olim hadashim receive considerable financial aid from the government.

Old City: the old quarter of Jerusalem, where all three major monotheistic religions—Judaism, Christianity, and Islam—have sacred sites.

Palestine: the modern name for the biblical Holy Land. The Jews call it Eretz Yisrael, the land of Israel; the Arabs, Filastine. In her letter, Mervet referred to Palestine before 1948. For more details see the historical section.

pogrom: anti-Semitic non-Jews would enter a Jewish village and kill all the residents that they could find.

Purim: the Jewish holiday that celebrates the thwarting of Minister Haman's plans to exterminate the Jews in ancient Persia. The holiday is celebrated by exchanging gifts, doing charitable acts, and eating cookies called hamantaschen (Haman's ear). Children wear costumes to the synagogue for the reading of the story.

Ramadan: the ninth month of the Muslim lunar calendar. For the whole month, Muslims keep a fast from sunrise to sunset. At night, families and friends gather to enjoy a traditional meal.

refugee camps: temporary camps for the Palestinians who lost their homes as a result of the War of Independence of 1948. For the most part, the refugees live under very precarious circumstances, crowded in small houses without running water, which have replaced tents and tin shacks. The exact number of Palestinian refugees is unknown. Estimates of 2.6 million include 350,000 in Lebanon, 300,000 in Syria, and 1.8 million in Jordan. Some live in camps, while others are integrated into the cities.

In the West Bank and Gaza: out of 1,800,000 residents in these territories occupied by Israel since 1967, one million are Palestinian refugees. The largest camps are Jabalya (80,000), Rafah (73,000), and Chatti (63,000).

Sabra: a prickly pear. This delicious fruit, which grows on a prickly pear cactus, is a name for Israelis who were born in the country. The symbolism is that the prickly outside hides a sweet, soft interior.

Saddam Hussein: the president of Iraq since 1979. On August 2, 1990, he invaded Kuwait, which started the Gulf War. In less than ten hours, Iraq occupied the country, sowing terror among the civilians and taking control of 40 percent of the world's petroleum resources. Defying the West and mocking international law, Saddam Hussein annexed Kuwait. The UN gave him an ultimatum: by January 15, 1991, his troops had to be out of Kuwait. A coalition of twenty-eight Western countries and some Arab countries, in particular Saudi Arabia, Egypt, and Syria, mobilized in the region. But Saddam stayed entrenched and threatened to bomb Israel with chemical weapons if war was declared. He hoped to transform the international conflict into an Israeli-Arab conflict and increase the provocation of Israel. If Israel responded, the coalition with the Arab countries would probably fall apart.

January 15, 1991, was the final day of the ultimatum. The coalition launched Operation Desert Storm. It was war. Scud missiles fell on Israel and Saudi Arabia. After twenty-four days of intense combat, the Iraqi troops fled Kuwait. Iraq was beaten, its economy in shambles and its people exhausted.

sealed room: during the Gulf War, Israel worried that the missiles launched against it carried chemical weapons. The Israeli civil defense counseled all Israelis to create a room in the interior of their homes that was hermetically sealed to make a shelter against toxic gas. The doors and windows were sealed with sheets of plastic taped to the frames. The floor was covered with rags soaked in water and bicarbonate. In case of an alert—which happened just about every night—entire families closed themselves into these rooms, put on gas masks, and waited for the all-clear signal.

settlers: Jewish citizens of Israel who live in the territories occupied by Israel since the Six-Day War in 1967. They have built homes in villages and fortified cities known as settlements. The settlers promote the annexation of the occupied territories on the basis that God promised the land to their ancestors in biblical times. One hundred and twenty thousand settlers live in the West Bank and in the Gaza Strip. Most are Orthodox Jews and ultranationalists. They are the core of the Israeli right wing.

Shabbat: the seventh day of the week for Jews is Saturday, a sacred day. They are required to observe a day of rest and are not allowed to light a fire. In modern times, observant Jews do not use any electricity, drive a car, or use a telephone, among other restrictions. According to the Bible, Shabbat is the day God rested after creating the world. Shabbat begins at sundown on Friday and ends when three stars appear in the sky on Saturday night.

shekel: Israeli money also used by Palestinians in the occupied territories.

small stones: Jews do not put flowers on graves. Instead, they leave small stones to indicate that the deceased are not forgotten.

synagogue: the religious building where Jews go to pray under the direction of a rabbi.

territories/occupied territories: the West Bank and Gaza Strip. The Israelis call them the territories or Judea and Samaria. The Palestinians call them the occupied territories. They are the land the Israelis won in the Six-Day War in 1967. Gaza is no longer under Israeli occupation.

Tiberias: a two-thousand-year-old city in Galilee. It rises from a lake, the Sea of Galilee. Tiberias is a popular tourist destination.

traitors or collaborators: Palestinians who help the Israelis buy land for Jewish settlers or who help Israelis arrest Palestinian activists. When a collaborator is discovered, he is killed. In four years, several hundred Palestinians accused of being collaborators have been murdered by militant Palestinians.

Tsahal: the Israeli army. At age eighteen, all Israelis, male and female, are called to perform required military service. See *milouim*.

UNRWA (United Nations Relief and Works Agency): organization created by the United Nations in 1949 to administer aid to the Palestinian refugees in the areas of employment, education, and the distribution of food.

TIMELINE

1897—First International Jewish Congress
1917—British conquest of Palestine and the Balfour
      Declaration
1929—Arab riots in Hebron
1936—Arab Revolt
1937—The Peel Commission
1939—MacDonald White Paper
1947—UN Resolution 181 divides Palestine between the
      Arabs and Jews
1948—State of Israel is established
      War of Independence: Egypt, Syria, Lebanon, and
      Jordan attack Israel.
1949—Cease-fire agreement ends War of Independence;
      Jerusalem is divided between Jordan and Israel.
1956—War between Egypt and Israel
1964—Palestine Liberation Organization (PLO) formed
1967—Six-Day War; Israel acquires territory, including
      part of Jerusalem formerly under Jordanian
      control.
1969—Yassir Arafat elected chairman of the PLO
1973—The Yom Kippur War
1977—Anwar el-Sadat, president of Egypt, visits Jerusalem
1978—Menachem Begin, prime minister of Israel, and
      Sadat win Nobel Peace Prize
1979—Camp David peace accord between Israel and
      Egypt is signed
1981—Sadat assassinated
1987—Intifada begins
1990—The Gulf War

1991—Peace negotiations between Israel, Palestine, Jordan, Syria, and Lebanon in Madrid, Spain

1993—Israeli-Palestinian negotiations in Oslo, Norway

Israeli-Palestinian Accord signed in Washington, D.C.; provides guidelines for Palestinian autonomy in territories conquered by Israel in Six-Day War

1994—Nobel Peace Prize awarded to Yassir Arafat, Yitzhak Rabin, prime minister of Israel, and Shimon Peres, Israeli foreign minister

Arafat sworn in as head of the Palestinian National Authority

Israel and Jordan end declared state of war

1995—Rabin assassinated; Peres becomes prime minister.

1996—Binyamin Netanyahu elected prime minister of Israel

Peace negotiations with Arafat resume

SUGGESTED READING

Ashrawi, Hanan. *This Side of Peace: A Personal Account.* New York: Simon & Schuster, 1995.

Chacour, Elias, with Mary E. Jensen. *We Belong to the Land: The Story of a Palestinian Israeli Who Lives for Peace and Reconciliation.* San Francisco: HarperSan Francisco, 1990.

Ciment, James. *Palestine/Israel: The Long Conflict.* New York: Facts on File, 1997.

Corzine, Phyllis. *The Palestinian-Israeli Accord.* San Diego, Calif.: Lucent Books, Inc., 1996.

Dudley, William, ed. *The Middle East: Opposing Viewpoints.* San Diego, Calif.: Greenhaven Press, 1992.

Grossman, David. *Sleeping on a Wire: Conversations with Palestinians in Israel.* New York: Farrar, Straus & Giroux, 1993.

Peres, Shimon. *Battling for Peace: A Memoir.* New York: Random House, 1995.

Peters, Joan. *From Time Immemorial: The Origins of the Arab-Jewish Conflict over Palestine.* New York: Harper & Row, 1984.

Richler, Mordecai. *This Year in Jerusalem.* New York: Knopf, 1994.

Shipler, David K. *Arab and Jew: Wounded Spirits in a Promised Land.* New York: Times Books, 1986.

Wallach, John and Janet. *Still Small Voices: The Untold Human Stories Behind the Violence on the West Bank and Gaza.* San Diego, Calif.: Harcourt Brace Jovanovich, 1989.

INDEX